sona

BOOKS

First published in the UK 2020 by Sona Books
an imprint of Danann Publishing Ltd.

Editor: Dan Peel, Hitesh Ratna
Copy Editor: Tom O'Neill
Contributors: David Luiz, Robert Pires, Gabriel Jesus, Xabi Alonso, Michael Owen, Jesse Lingard,
Javi, Martinez, Dominic Calvert-Lewin and many more...

CAT NO: **SON0458**
ISBN: **978-1-912918-13-3**

Made in EU.

soccer

PLAY LIKE A PRO

contents

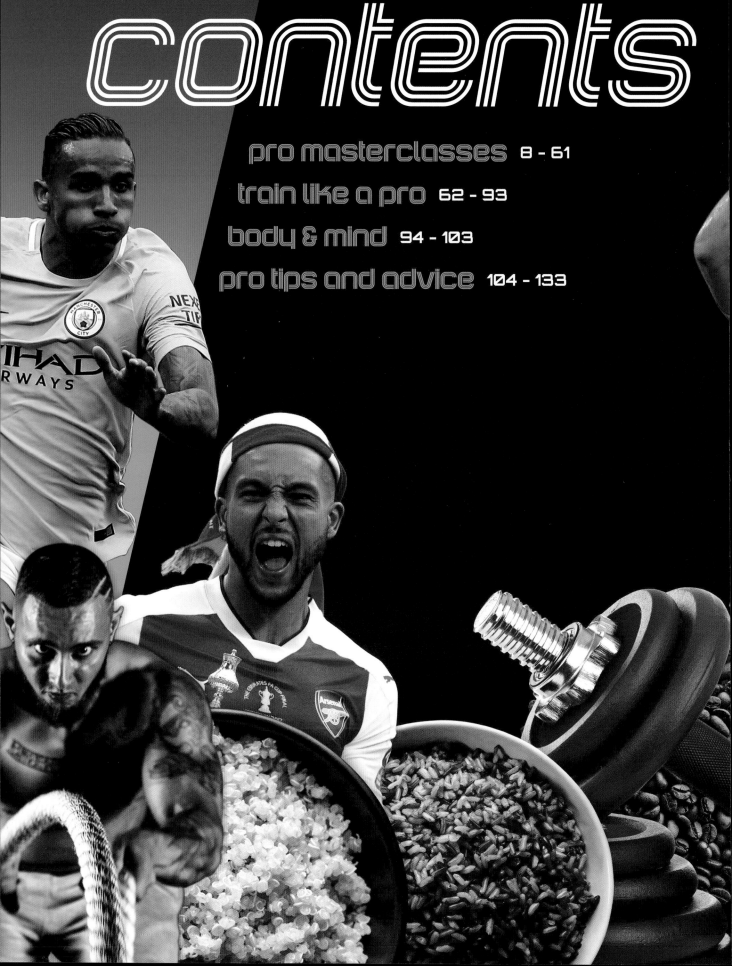

pro masterclasses 8 - 61

train like a pro 62 - 93

body & mind 94 - 103

pro tips and advice 104 - 133

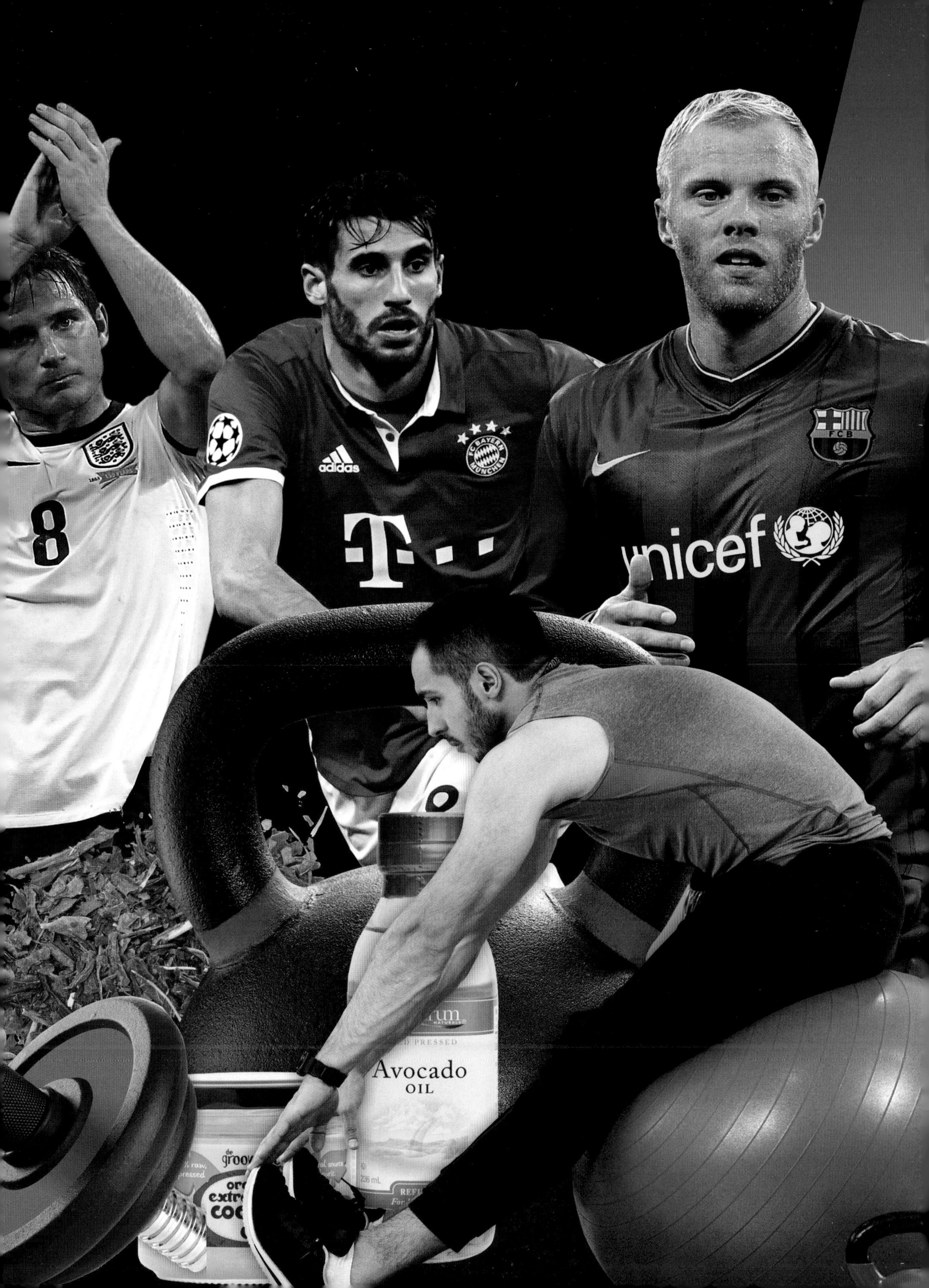
8
adidas
FC BAYERN MÜNCHEN
FCB
unicef
PRESSED
Avocado
OIL

pro masterclasses

FERNANDINHO

Man City's midfield dynamo on playing under Pep, keeping it simple and idolising

Which central midfielders did you admire when you were growing up?

As a kid I played for a side called PSTC (Parana Soccer Technical Center) from Londrina, and in those days we didn't have a professional team, just a youth team. So the primary objective of that club was to develop talented players. One of the main players who left and became successful was Kleberson. He won the 2002 World Cup and played for Manchester United, so he became an example for every young player at the club to follow. Back then, he was the guy that inspired me, and he was a big reason why I decided to become a central midfielder. I was also lucky enough to play in the same team as him for Atletico Paranaense.

Have you always been deployed as a defensive midfielder?

Not always. I played in more attacking positions at the beginning of my career. I spent a bit of time as a second striker and even a winger, too, because I was younger and faster. As time passed by, I started to move back down the pitch, especially when I went to Ukraine with Shakhtar Donetsk. The manager played me as a second midfielder, as we say in Brazil, in the box-to-box role. When I joined Man City I played even deeper, really close to the central defenders, as the first man in the midfield. My history of playing in different areas began long before I even became a professional, to be honest. The only position I've never played in is goalkeeper!

Does a top holding midfielder need to have an unselfish streak?

I think so, yes. It's great to score a goal or set one up occasionally, but I believe that my main function in the team is to provide balance between attacking and defending. When I first started playing football, my managers always told me that the midfielders were the heart and lungs of the team, and I needed to feed the other sectors of the field. That was something I always took with me, and even now I try to do that when I'm out on the pitch.

How important is positioning if you are playing this role?

It's a huge part of a holding midfielder's game. Our most basic function is to get closer to the opposition and reduce the amount of space they've got to play in. Today, football's a lot more compact. It is different compared to when I started out back in Brazil. In the modern game, defensive midfielders end up playing in a distance that's no greater than, let's say, 20 metres from the defensive line to the attacking line, where the striker is. It's such a short space, with all of the players close together, so this makes it easier for me to cover plenty of ground and close people down.

Have your responsibilities under Pep Guardiola (below) changed compared to previous managers?

I've learned exceptional things from the manager about my position, specifically about when to take the ball forward and the importance of respecting the space of my team-mates. A lot of the time, the opposing side will try to press us using three attacking players. That means I have to find the right time and space to get the ball back and quickly give it to one of the midfielders in front of me. Obviously you analyse the opponent before the game, but things can change very quickly once you are on the field. Guardiola teaches his players in such a way that they are able to adapt to any changes instantly and independently.

Can it be quite difficult to understand his style of football?

No, not at all. A lot of people think that, because of the way his teams played at Barcelona, Bayern Munich and now City, he must ask some extraordinary things of his players – but he doesn't. Pep just wants the game to be played as simply as possible. Our game is based on two touches. All you need to understand is that he doesn't want his players to run 15 or 20 metres – he wants us to move three or four metres. Then we can open up a space and find some passing lines to receive the ball, play a quick one-two and speed up the game. In Brazil, and other European countries, players end up touching the ball many times before making their pass, but at City we try to touch it as little as possible so that the ball moves around fast.

You've played as a centre-back a few times under Guardiola – what does he demand of his defenders?

I think being a defender in a Guardiola team is one of the toughest things you can do in football. You've got to be able to see openings, have excellent passing ability and act fast, as there's a massive space behind you that allows the other team to score on the break if you make a mistake. It's been very cool watching our defenders participating in offensive plays, creating chances and starting off team attacks from our penalty area. But it's very important that we all remember our defensive duties at the same time. It's tough being a defender under Guardiola, so our defenders deserve to be congratulated this season!

> "A lot of people think Pep must ask extraordinary things of players, but he doesn't – he wants to see the game played simply and fast"

THE DETAILS

The Samba star reveals his selfless superpower and F1 icon

Worst habit
Using my smartphone too much

Favourite film
Gladiator

Childhood hero
Ayrton Senna (top)

Dream dinner guest
Denzel Washington

Favourite sports
F1, volleyball, basketball and American football

Favourite band
Revelacao

Phone wallpaper
A photo of me with my wife and kids

If you could have a secret power...
I'd end all of the hunger in the world

Favourite TV show
The news

Signature dish
Lasagne

Interview Ulisses Neto

DAVID LUIZ

Chelsea's Samba star on pre-match prep, coping with criticism and the role of the modern defender

Hi David. You seem to have a very laid-back personality – how do you remain so relaxed during a match?

I'm anything but relaxed! But thanks, I'm happy you think that. When you play at this level of football there's no room to be relaxed for any second at all. As a Chelsea player, I am involved in top-level competitions for the entire season and my level of concentration is just as high as my responsibilities. The day before a match I am already living it. I think about the game, plan my strategy, focus on my opponent's ability and so on. This thought process continues right until the final whistle of the match and it soon starts again in preparation for the following game.

Some players describe suffering from pre-match nerves – is this something you've experienced?

The most important thing is to forget everything that surrounds you away from football and simply focus on the manager's advice. If you have got his confidence and your team-mates' as well, it's all you need to go and show your quality on the pitch. Facing tough moments throughout the 90 minutes is a part of the game, but you have to remain focused and forget about any particular mistake that might happen. If you manage to do so and stay calm, you will end up avoiding bad decisions.

Gary Neville said that you played as if 'being controlled by a 10-year-old on a PlayStation' during a defeat to Liverpool in 2011. Did that hurt you?

I prefer to give attention to constructive criticism. I respond well to that sort of feedback because I can learn from it and improve in the future. This type of advice makes you reflect on your game and informs you how to improve from mistakes you may have made. Helpful advice, which comes from polite people – like family and friends as well as your coaches and team-mates – is always very welcome. I get stronger with this kind of criticism. It helps to make me a better player and better person, too.

You're a centre-back who likes to get on the ball a lot. How did you learn to become so comfortable in possession?

This comes from my time in the youth teams of Vitoria, back in Brazil. I used to play as a holding midfielder there and developed this taste for getting the ball and trying to start an attack whenever it was possible. I practised how to control the ball, keep hold of it and pass it well over short and long distances. All of these skills are really important regardless of your position in the team's formation. I've utilised these attributes at every club that I've played for since then and tried to show it in each competition. I'm always

trying to improve my skills and correct mistakes during training sessions. Nothing comes for free.

Do you think the role of a defender has evolved recently?

Yes, it's definitely changed because football as a whole has changed as well. But at the end of the day, your duties will always depend on your manager's decisions. The centre-back's role usually gets affected by the system that your team uses and the strategy you have, so it will be different for every club. In some systems there's more freedom for a defender to go forward, but in others you have got to stay back all of the time. Also, in the past it was pretty rare to see defenders taking a curling free-kick, as they'd always be really powerful shots. However, now we see players hitting the ball like forwards and midfielders, right?

> "The day before a match starts I'm already living it. I plan strategy and focus on my opponents until the final whistle"

Do you prefer to play as a holding midfielder or a central defender?

I prefer to do whatever the manager wants. At the moment I'm playing as a sweeper for Chelsea, although I did play in front of the centre-backs during my first spell at the club. It all depends on the manager's decision, which can also be impacted by the strengths and weaknesses of our opponents. For me, it isn't difficult to adapt to a new role. As a professional footballer you must be ready to fight for your team-mates, no matter where you are on the pitch.

How big a challenge was it adapting to European football when you joined Benfica, after growing up in Brazil?

I believe that the culture of the country influences its style of football. You carry the values you learn off the pitch onto it as well. In general, players from Europe have more discipline in comparison to the South American players. On the other hand, improvising may come more naturally to the South Americans. However, this is changing because of the huge number of South American players now in Europe, which means that both cultures are influencing one another. But some differences will continue to exist and, as a Brazilian, I have to admit that it's an advantage if you have the ability to improvise during the difficult moments.

THE DETAILS

The Blues' boy from Brazil has proved pretty handy in both penalty areas

Age
31

Height
6ft 3in

Birthplace
Diadema

Shirt number
30

Chelsea games
223

Chelsea goals
16

Brazil games
56

Brazil goals
3

*Up to January 10, 2019

Interview Felipe Rocha

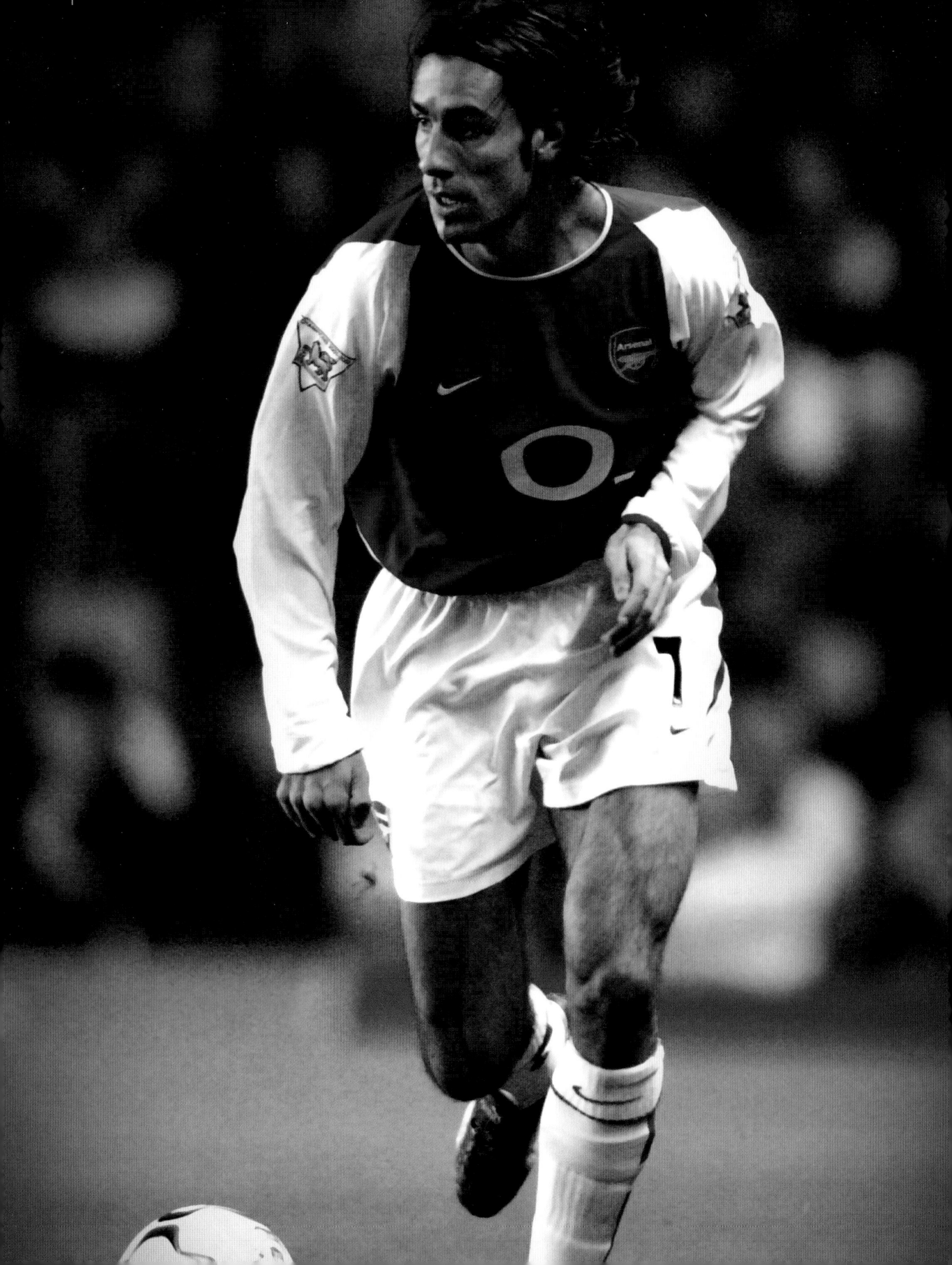
Arsenal

ROBERT PIRES

The legendary Arsenal man reveals how he wreaked havoc as an inverted winger

You're right-footed but played on the left. How did you end up in that role?

I had come through as a youngster in France playing as a left-winger, so was already comfortable in that role before I moved to the Premier League. When I joined Arsenal from Marseille in 2000, Arsene Wenger told me, "You're going to play on the left wing to replace Marc Overmars. Do you think you're capable of playing on that side?" As I knew the position I replied, "Yes, I feel like I can replace him." I remember fans being really confused and saying things like, "Why is Pires playing on the left when he is right-footed?" Your relationship with your coach is really important at times like this. He needs to know you are confident in your ability and that you're totally at ease in that position.

> "My toughest opponent? My old friend Gary Neville. He was not a dirty player, but he gave me plenty of kicks!"

Is it an advantage to be able to cut inside onto your stronger foot?

As a right-footer on the left wing, you have got a 'broader palette', as we say in French. When you start to run infield from that position, you are able to see the entire game laid out in front of you. As an inverted winger you are on your stronger foot, so you're obviously a lot more comfortable as well. When you drift infield you can supply passes to players inside you and to the strikers, or you can just get forward and score yourself. Those are a few reasons why the role was so intriguing for me when I joined Arsenal. It's more common for teams to play with an inverted winger these days. At the time I had to work really hard on it with Arsene Wenger in training – and you saw the results.

Thierry Henry (right) says you were a master of 'freezing' defenders – what exactly does he mean by this?

Speed wasn't my strongest asset, so I had to rely on other qualities to try to get the better of my opponents in one-on-one situations. My signature move was the stop-start dribble. I'd set off, stop and then set off again to beat a player. It came naturally to me. When I saw it was

effective, I continued to work at it on the training pitch. I ended up using that move quite a lot during my time in England. This is a really good example of the fact that you must work on your strong points as well as your weak ones. Perfecting your technique when you know that you're good at something is very important.

Did you ever feel that you could been effective playing in the No.10 role?

I think I could have been a success as a central playmaker – but it was from the left-wing position that I was best able to display my qualities. I learned a lot about the No.10 role while playing alongside Dennis Bergkamp for Arsenal. Then when I was called up to join the France team, Zinedine Zidane was the No.10 and the same happened with him: he taught me all about the position just through me watching him. In the same way, players can learn the role today by looking at Mesut Özil and the way he plays in that position for Arsenal.

Who was the toughest full-back that you ever faced in the Premier League?

It's very easy to name my most difficult opponent – my old friend Gary Neville! The games against Manchester United were always difficult when I was playing against him. When he was on the pitch they were physically, but also mentally, difficult fixtures. He would try to provoke me. He gave me plenty of kicks, but that is part of the game in England. He was not a dirty player – he was just a good right-back. He'd always do his best for Man United and I always did my best for Arsenal, so there was a great deal of respect between the two of us. Who came out on top overall? To be honest, he usually got the better of me during our battles. I would say it was probably about 60-40 in favour of Gary Neville.

Former Leeds defender Danny Mills said that you introduced diving to the Premier League - is that unfair?

Really? I have no issue with him saying that if that's what he thinks, but I was no cheat. If you get kicked, eventually you end up on the ground. It's not my fault if he was clumsy, is it? The ref is out there to judge whether a foul has been committed or if it was simulation. As far as the physical side of English football goes, you have to be able to adapt to your surroundings. I used to receive plenty of knocks from the likes of Mills – and Rio Ferdinand too – but you have to get on with it. It's part of the game.

THE DETAILS

Pires by numbers

2000
Arsenal debut

198
Premier League appearances

115
Premier League wins

62
Premier League goals

41
Premier League assists

2
Premier League titles

3
FA Cups

79
France caps

14
France goals

1
World Cup

1
European Championship

Interview James Eastham

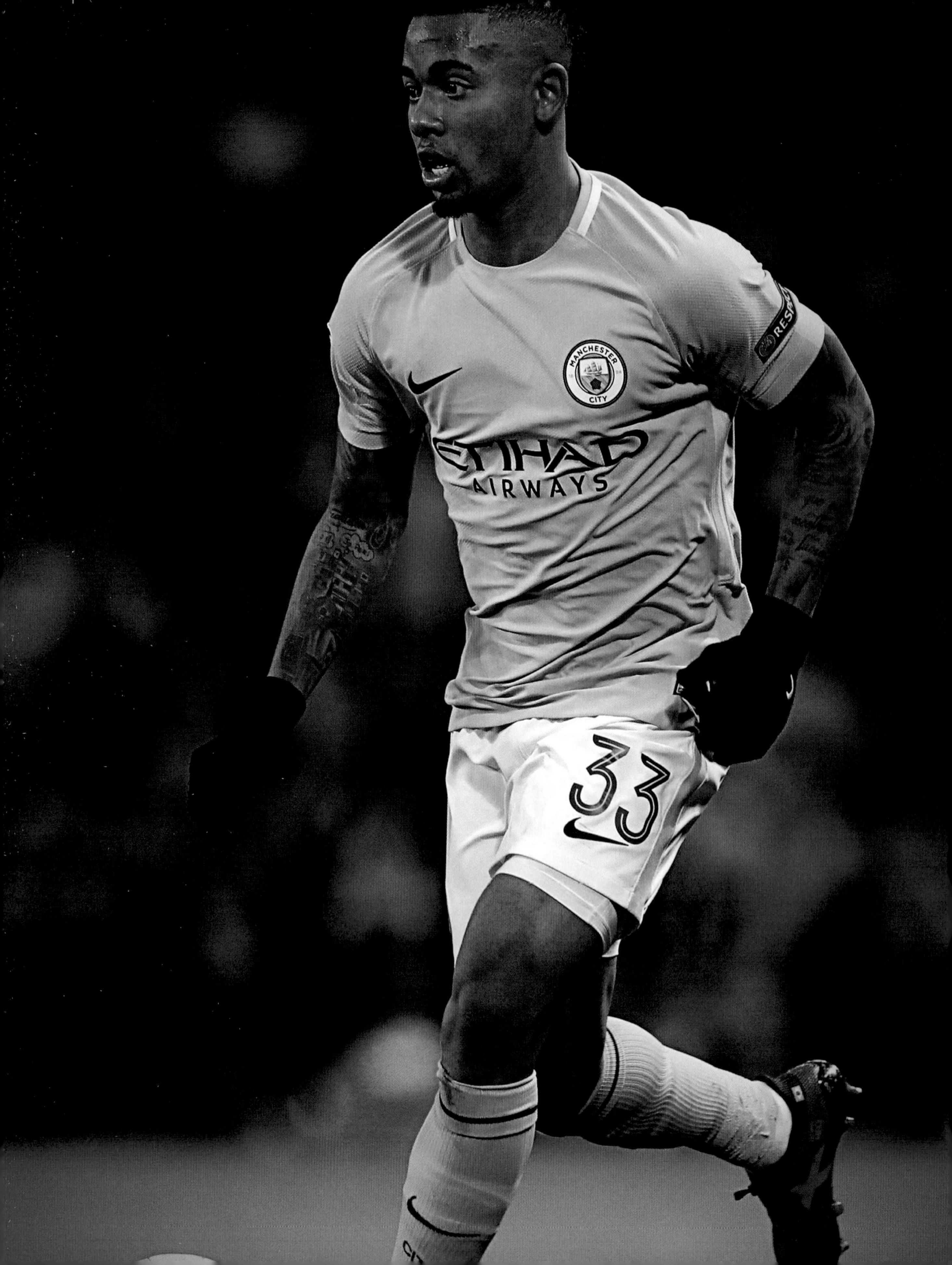
MANCHESTER CITY
ETIHAD AIRWAYS
33

GABRIEL JESUS

The Manchester City striker on staying calm in front of goal, toning down trickery and the need for speed

Some of Brazil's finest players honed their skills out on the streets – were you the same?

Yes, street football helped me a lot when I was younger. I learnt technical skills in really tight spaces, but I also learnt how to fight and battle, which were equally important. My experiences playing street football meant I was no longer afraid of facing a tackle on the pitch. Sometimes it was a bit dangerous, but it was worth it as I learnt to fight for what I wanted, and always with honesty. Whenever I'm playing now, I can still feel the benefits of street football.

Who were your favourite Samba stars when you were growing up?

The players I watched the most as a kid were Ronaldo and Ronaldinho. I obviously know Romario as well from watching lots of videos of him, and I still do that now and again. It's just a shame for me that I wasn't able to watch him play when he was at his peak, although I know how talented he was. Brazil have produced so many incredible attacking players over the years, but those three are the ones I admire.

Those three players were so relaxed in the final third. How do you develop that calmness in pressure situations?

It's hard to explain that. I guess at some point you kind of develop this quality of being calm. When I graduated from the Palmeiras youth team to the first team, I got so nervous in these situations. I've managed to improve that, but I'm still young. Sometimes I can stay calm and on other occasions I can't – it's normal. I'll get better at this area of my game as I grow older and gain more experience; you continue to learn throughout your career. I don't think it's a quality that all Brazilian players possess, though. There are many Brazilians players who aren't relaxed in the final third!

In Brazil you would beat players with tricks and flicks – have you changed since moving to England?

From the moment I started playing as a forward, I stopped dribbling as much as I did on the flanks. I am much more direct these days and simply try to get in the penalty box and score. Whenever I played out wide, I always liked to cut inside and do loads of stepovers. I still enjoy doing lots of tricks, but now I'm focused on scoring goals because that's what wins matches.

You've adapted to English football so quickly since joining Manchester City in 2017. Do you believe it's easier to adjust now due to the high number of South Americans there?

I wouldn't say that. I feel it's more to do with my style of play, as I like to battle, fight and give everything for every ball. These are the things that helped me the most when I joined City from Palmeiras. I already had these characteristics when I was in Brazil so they were useful when I started playing in England, where there is more contact compared to other European countries.

Pace is key to the way you play – can you be a top attacker in the modern game without a quick pair of heels?

Good question. To be honest, there are many attacking players who aren't that quick and they're still able to score goals. It's also true that football has changed a lot and the game now demands more from you. In the past, there were many players who weren't quick, but they were technically so good and clinical that they found the back of the net anyway. Nowadays, I'd say it's more difficult for these strikers to reach the top, because the defenders are also fast. I think you need speed to be a successful forward at the highest level of the game.

> "When I played out wide, I'd cut inside and do lots of stepovers. I still enjoy doing tricks, but now I'm focused on scoring goals"

Do today's frontmen also need to be able to play in several positions, and which is your favourite?

Definitely. I think this is very important, because formations are more flexible in modern football. It means you can end up playing in various areas of the final third, regardless of your position at the start of a match. It's a great advantage for me to play in at least three different positions – that can only be good for my development. I used to like playing out wide, but I've been playing as a striker with Brazil and City for over a year now and I'm really enjoying it – I see myself as a striker at the moment.

Should a forward go for placement or power when shooting at goal?

It's relative, because it depends on how you like shooting in different situations. In my case, I prefer to go for accuracy rather than more power. If you have the ability to score with accurate shots, you don't necessarily need to blast the ball at the target every time. The harder you kick it, the harder it is to be accurate and find the corners of the goal. You are hoping that the speed of the ball will be enough to beat the keeper. Of course, there are a few occasions when you've got to put some power on your shot to score. To do that you strike the ball using your laces, although I personally prefer to use the inside part of my feet whenever I get a chance to pull the trigger.

THE DETAILS

City's Samba star has had a hand in 32 league goals from only 55 appearances

Age
21

Height
5ft 9in

Birthplace
Sao Paulo

Man City debut
January 2017

League games
55

Goals
23

Assists
9

Shot accuracy
57%

Brazil caps
24

Goals
11

*Up to January 10, 2019

Interview Felipe Rocha

XABI ALONSO

The pass master teaches you about game intelligence and learning from other sports

THE DETAILS

The business buff picks his proudest day and big regrets

Which of the game's great passers did you like to watch as a youngster?
I think that Pep Guardiola and Lothar Matthaus were two of the great passers of their generation and I watched them a lot. Paul Scholes was also a wonderful player and someone I really respected, and in the modern game Toni Kroos is now one of the world's best passers.

When did you realise that passing had become your area of expertise?
As soon as I started playing football, passing was something that just came very naturally to me. My game wasn't about dribbling or getting the ball and scoring many goals; it was about being in the middle of the pitch, it was about spreading the ball from one side of the pitch to the other, using short passes and long passes. That was my game.

Do you think a sweetly-struck pass is as satisfying as scoring a goal?
It feels great. As soon as I hit the ball, I know if it's going to be a good ball or a bad one. I've got to know the feeling on my foot so well that within the first millisecond I know if I have hit it right. When it travels at the right speed and height and then arrives at the correct moment to help a team-mate, I love it.

How did you go about honing your passing ability over your career?
The quality of my passing when I was a 20-year-old and the way that I pass the ball at 35 is exactly the same, but the difference is my understanding of the game. I'm more mature now and know how to distribute the ball better in different situations, but I don't think the passing itself changes that much.

Did you have to change your passing style for different types of players?
Yes. It's crucial for me to know to who I am passing to. Some players want the ball to feet, others want it in space. One player might want the ball played into him on his right foot, whereas another prefers it on his left foot. These small details can all make a huge difference, and you need to give your team-mate an advantage. This is something that has come to me naturally because I've been in the game for such a long time.

How did you manage to find so much space in midfield to hit those passes?
It's about trying to anticipate what is going to happen and what you have to do. This will help to give you more time on the ball. If you're only just starting to think about what you're going to do when the ball arrives at your feet, it's already too late. You need to know your space. If you understand this, then you don't have to run around too much because you run smarter.

> "For me, passing is as good as scoring a goal – it was never my job to put the ball in the back of the net"

Did you ever look at any other sports to try to improve your striking of the ball?
Yes. I like watching and playing other sports where there is a ball involved. It doesn't matter if the ball is smaller or bigger than a football – I can still relate to it. The coordination and striking skills transfer to football as well. I like playing tennis and basketball and occasionally golf, too. I'm not great at it but I'd like to learn and get better. All of those sports require that feel for the ball whenever you connect with it.

Did you prefer to be in a midfield that played a short or direct passing game?
It depended on who I was playing for. I can remember one week when I was at Real Madrid and in front of me there was Cristiano Ronaldo, Angel Di Maria, Gareth Bale and Karim Benzema. They love the ball being played into space so they can run onto it, because they have those qualities. Three days later I was training alongside Andres Iniesta, Xavi and David Silva for Spain, and that was more about combinations, small passes and creating 3 vs 2 situations to gain an advantage. It wasn't about space and counter-attack. You need to know your team-mates – that changes everything.

You must have hit tens of thousands of passes during your career – are there any that are your favourites?
I have hit a few good ones over the years so it's quite tough to pick out just one or two! What I would say is that, for me, passing is as good as scoring a goal. It was never my job to go and put the ball in the back of the net. It was about giving the ball to my team-mates who'd then do that, and it is something I have always loved to do.

Alonso was speaking at a UEFA Champions League Trophy Tour event at Adidas' store on Oxford Street.

Interview Alec Fenn

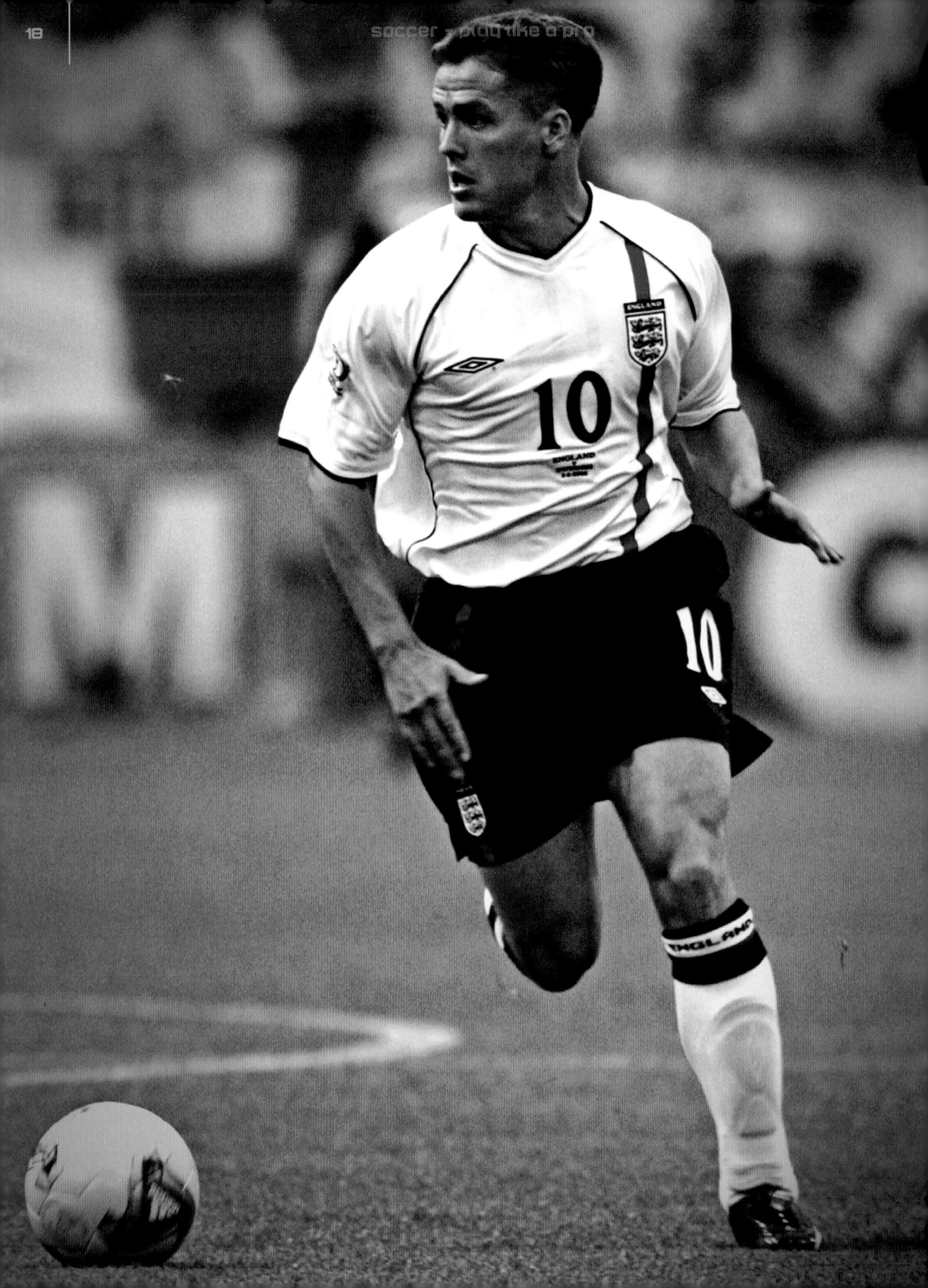
10
ENGLAND
10

MICHAEL OWEN

The former Liverpool and England marksman shares his blueprint on how to create the perfect goalscorer

Hi Michael. Do you believe goalscorers are born or made?

I think it's a bit of both, to be honest. To be a goalscorer you have to be a certain type of person. You've got to be selfish and have an obsessive streak, which are both personality traits I believe you're born with. Improving your goalscoring is all about quality practice and having the chance to work on your finishing in matches over and over again.

What's the best way for a forward to develop their finishing?

I have a clear idea about how to create a world-class goalscorer. In the modern game, a lot of young players are moved up an age group in their academies to challenge them. They'll still be good in that age group, so they'll be pushed up again. Eventually it gets too difficult for them – they don't have enough chances in front of goal to practise their craft. If you only get one opportunity per game, you'll favour your tried-and-tested finish every time and never build a repertoire.

When I was at school, I'd get about 15 chances per game and often score nine goals. I quickly figured out the finishes that worked well for me and those that didn't. But to do that, you need to have loads and loads of chances to practise different goalscoring situations until it's instinctive. You can only do that if you're continually playing at a level that allows you to dominate and have opportunities in front of goal.

Would you say academies produce as many goalscorers today compared to when you rose through Liverpool's ranks in the '90s?

No. Since Jose Mourinho bought Didier Drogba in 2004 and Chelsea started to win titles with a lone striker, the position has changed completely. The stereotypical centre-forward now is a big lad who can do everything. When I was coming through, there were twice as many strikers because everyone played with two guys up top. We would practise a lot of combination play and operating with a big man and a little man. It didn't matter what shape or size you were, you could be a striker. These days, if you're not a certain size, there's no point being a striker because you won't be able to play that role. I'd find it really hard coming through now if I had to keep winning high balls, hold the ball up and do everything.

Which types of finishes did you enjoy applying the most?

If you look back over my career, I rarely rounded the goalkeeper, as I just didn't like that finish. I tried it dozens of times when I was a kid and it didn't come off too often. I soon discovered that I liked either curling the ball into the corner or opening up my body and side-footing it home from a certain angle. I also used to be good at pushing the ball in front of me, so the goalkeeper thought I'd taken a heavy touch and would come off his line. But it was actually deliberate, as I knew that I could use my pace to beat him to the ball and then dink it over him as he raced out and dived at my feet. If I was one-on-one with the goalkeeper, I'd usually try to position him

where I wanted him to be. I always liked to run onto the ball at an angle, because I could move the keeper and then open up the space to slot it past him and into the bottom corner.

Can you learn to keep a cool head in one-on-one situations?

Yes. You need to have experienced many one-on-one situations to develop that calmness when you're through on goal. A very good example of this is Mohamed Salah's goal for Liverpool in last season's Champions League quarter-final second leg at Manchester City. Before that goal, I had him down as a player who missed quite a few chances and didn't always pick the right finish. However, the more opportunities he's been given, the better he's become. He looked like an ice-cold finisher against Man City. If you're a top striker, your heart rate should slow down in these situations. Salah took an extra second and waited for the keeper to go down, before dinking the ball over him. That tells me his heart rate is decreasing in one-on-one situations.

> "I'd push the ball in front of me so the keeper came off his line. I knew I could beat him to it and then dink it over him"

You scored so many of your goals from through-balls - what would you do to exploit space?

If I didn't have the ball, I'd avoid filling an area that I wanted to exploit. I'd drop off a little bit so the defensive line would move higher and I could run in behind. I wanted defenders to think that I just wanted the ball to feet, but really I was sucking them in so that I could spin and burst away. The quickest route to goal is in a straight line from A to B, but you will probably keep getting caught offside by doing that. You need to position yourself between the full-back and centre-back, then bend the run and get the speed up.

Once you're in that position, keep your head up. Too many players don't look up until the keeper's only a few feet away. You're in possession of the ball, which means you're in control of the situation. Angle your run so you move the keeper exactly where you want him to be, and then you can pick your spot.

Owen was speaking on behalf of BT Sport

Interview Alec Fenn

THE DETAILS

At Euro 2004, he became the first man to score at four major tournaments for England

Birthplace
Chester

Premier League clubs
Liverpool, Newcastle, Man United, Stoke

Premier League appearances
326

Goals
150

Assists
31

Titles
1 (2010-11)

Golden Boot
1997-98 (18 goals)
1998-99 (18 goals)

England appearances
89

England goals
40

JESSE LINGARD

Manchester United's footloose forward tells you how to leave defenders in a spin

You've played in so many different positions for Manchester United. Which role suits you the best?

I think for now, playing on the wing and cutting inside – that's where I'll continue to play. However, over the next few years I would really like to become a No.10. I have played there a few times for England and United and that's my natural position. But while I'm still growing, playing out wide is good for my development.

Former Manchester United coach Rene Meulensteen compared you to Andres Iniesta a few years ago – what was your reaction to that?

I've always admired Andres Iniesta – the things he's done on the pitch are unbelievable. I have watched a lot of videos of him and looked at the way he plays. I wouldn't say I've copied what he does, but I certainly look at his style and want to take parts of his game and add them to my own.

You seem to have a knack for beating opposition players in tight spaces. Have you always been good at that?

Yeah, I would say from being a young player, I've always enjoyed dribbling with the ball, collecting the ball in tight spaces and then trying to make things happen. As I've developed it's become a really strong part of my game. I have managed to take that into my matches and cause problems for the opposition.

Physically, you are quite small in stature – were you ever worried that this would hold you back?

Yeah, at United it kind of did. When I was playing in the under-18 age group, I had to play under-16 level football. But United had always said to me that I was a late developer and that I just needed to be patient. They always thought I would be 22 or 23 before I broke through into the first team. Those were the words of Alex Ferguson. I always listened to him and trusted all of his words – now I'm a regular for Manchester United.

You have had several loans. Did you fear you wouldn't make it at United?

I just wanted to play football when I was younger – no matter what the level. It was all about the enjoyment of playing. Whether I was playing for the under-16s, 15s or 14s, it did not matter to me. Over the years I have developed, and after I played reserve football, that was when I really kicked on. I was sent out on loan – that was the classic Fergie development plan – and then I came back a better player.

Paul Scholes says you should score 15 goals a season. Do you agree?

Definitely. As soon as I heard him say that, I agreed with him. At youth level

I played in a great side, with players like Paul Pogba, Danny Drinkwater and Ravel Morrison, and in that team I scored a lot of goals. Last season I think I could have scored 10 goals and that's a big target of mine – I need to score more goals and get more assists.

> "I have always admired Andres Iniesta. I watch a lot of videos of him and want to add parts of his game to mine"

Did you admire any strikers when you were still learning the game?

Ruud van Nistelrooy was a big hero of mine when I was growing up. He was such an amazing finisher and scored so many different types of goals with both feet. The thing that set him apart was how calm he was when he was in front of goal. Wayne Rooney is another player that I would watch a lot when I was younger and I have been lucky enough to play with him at United. His overhead kick in the win against Manchester City [in 2011] is probably my favourite goal. To have the ability to produce that in a derby was just incredible. I still remember seeing it on TV at home and jumping up and down inside my living room.

Do you think that strikers need to have different personalities to other outfield players to succeed?

I think strikers need to have a certain type of personality to be successful. The team is always relying on them to put the ball in the back of the net. I think that the very best strikers really enjoy having that responsibility to win matches and get points for the team.

Goalscorers: are they born or made?

A lot of the great strikers that I have played with and watched have been natural goalscorers. Players such as Van Nistelrooy, Rooney and Dimitar Berbatov all have that killer instinct in front of goal. But I think all three of them combined that with a great work ethic to hone their ability. They all stayed on after training to practise different shooting drills and various situations that they would experience in a game.

Where do you see yourself in five years?

Hopefully I'll still be playing regularly for Man United – I want to be playing week in, week out and become established in the first team, and it would be nice to win lots of trophies as well.

THE DETAILS

Jesse's path from Fletcher Moss Ranger to Three Lion

Age
26

Height
5ft 9in

Birthplace
Warrington

Schoolboy club
Fletcher Moss Rangers – the same side that produced fellow United forwards Marcus Rashford & Danny Welbeck.

Man United debut
He started the 2-1 loss to Swansea in 2014, but had to come off injured after 24 minutes.

First United goal
Scored the opener in a 2-0 victory at home to West Brom in November 2015.

England debut
Started England's 2-0 win at home to Malta last October.

Favourite trick
"I love a nutmeg, but I've also been done by one this season."

Interview Alec Fenn

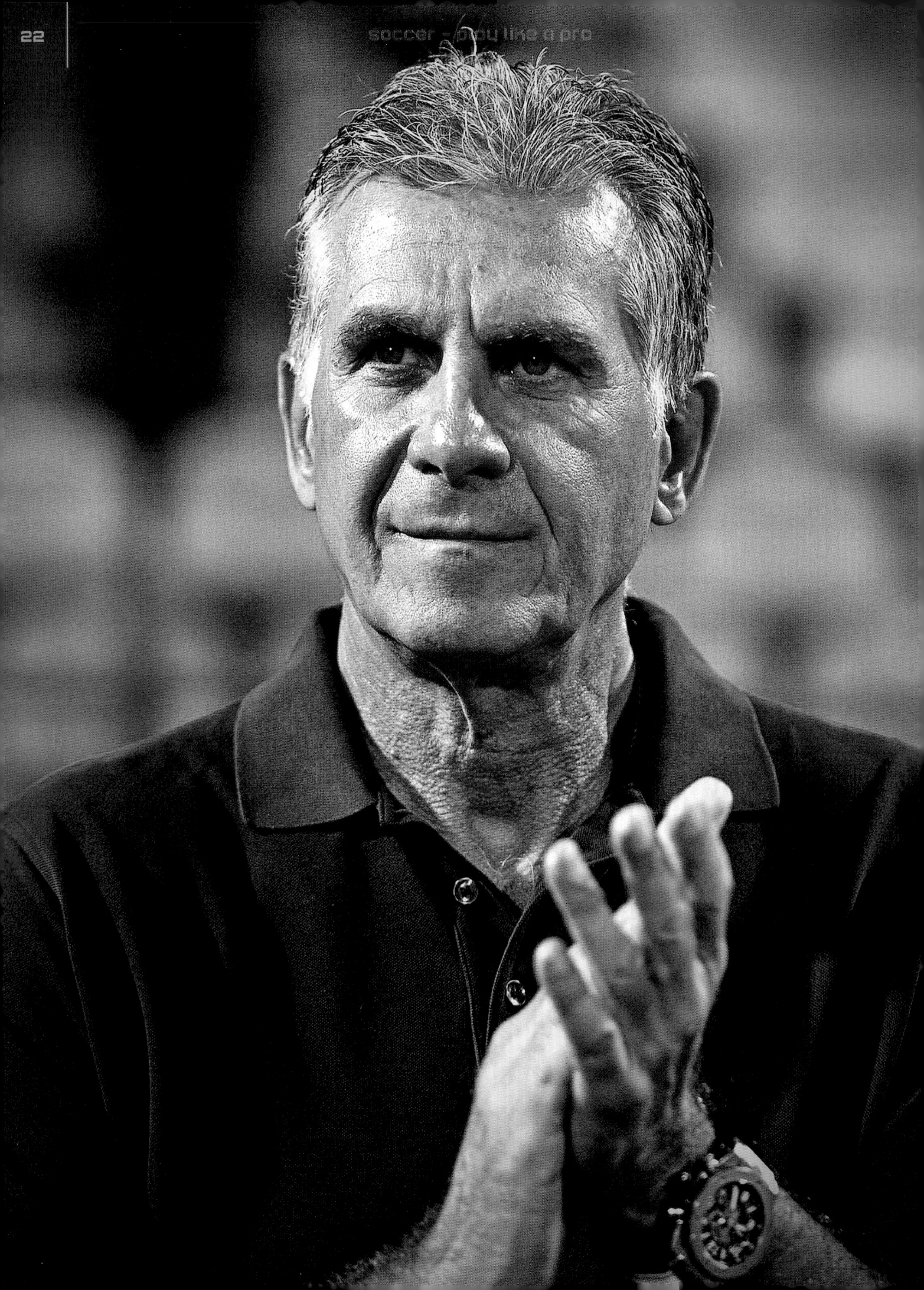

masterclass

CARLOS QUEIROZ

The Iran boss on young managers, the traits that great players share, and how to beat Barcelona

Carlos, you've been both a first-team coach and assistant manager. What is the difference between the roles?

I'd say the main difference between the two is responsibility. The manager is the leader and the one who's entrusted with making good decisions regarding every single aspect of the team. In both roles, you must not ignore your principles and always remain loyal.

You've been a coach since 1984. What tips would you give to the 30-year-old Carlos Queiroz at the beginning of his managerial career?

If I could give him one bit of advice, I'd tell him to try to stay in a positive mood at all times, regardless of what football throws at you during your career. That's a valuable piece of advice but also hard to follow because, despite what a lot of people think, being a manager is a very difficult and demanding job.

A lot of younger coaches are coming through at the top level these days - why do you think this is?

There isn't a secret recipe for becoming a successful manager. It all depends on the individual's ability to do the job well. I don't believe age is either a benefit or a negative aspect for having a career in this profession. What I do believe is that the success of a manager always comes from their knowledge, experiences and leadership, and these three factors have no relation to their age.

Have you had to alter your coaching style over the years, and do you work differently with modern footballers compared to previous generations?

Being a step ahead of your time is not just an obligation for every manager – it's the only possible way to success. If you really want to become a successful coach, adaptation is a non-negotiable characteristic that you must have and then develop. Every great manager in football history knew how to adapt to different situations on and off the pitch. Have I changed my style since my early days? The best coaches don't change - they just improve!

You have coached Cristiano Ronaldo, David Beckham and Zinedine Zidane. Do the greatest players share traits?

Definitely. They aren't the best players in the world because of magic, luck or anything else. They are who they are because of two crucial elements. First, an intelligent, systematic and intense manner in how they prepare for every training session and take care of their minds and bodies away from the pitch. The second, which I strongly believe in, is that super-athletes are mentally and psychologically stronger than normal athletes, and this difference means the greatest players are often a fraction of a second ahead of the others.

> "Super-athletes are mentally and psychologically stronger, so the greatest players are a fraction of a second ahead of the others"

You helped Alex Ferguson to produce a tactical masterclass when Manchester United faced Barcelona over two legs in the 2008 Champions League semi-finals. How did you get the players to understand your instructions?

The simple game has four crucial elements: space, time, number, and the harmonic mixture of all three. You will find some sides who are usually dominant in space, others in time, others in numbers. The quality of that specific Barcelona team made us believe that United could not approach the match focusing on number or time. So we planned to approach the semi-final trying to dominate the space element. This meant trying to control the zones of the pitch where Barcelona normally beat their opponents. In simple terms, we managed to occupy the key spaces of the pitch before Barça could use the same spaces to hurt us.

How were you able to deny Barcelona space in both legs, stay organised and maintain concentration?

The idea of what we wanted to achieve in the two games was the starting point for us. This meant we had very clearly decided what we wanted and needed to do. Then you have to work hard and pick the correct preparation methods to help get the job done – and that's what we did. We were completely sure about what we had to do against Barcelona, which was beating them by occupying the crucial spaces of the pitch. And we all understood that was something we could not give up or forget for a second of those 180 minutes.

Do you think some coaches are trying to over-complicate the game?

Yes. I'm not really a fan of this current tendency to intellectualise the game – football is a simple game. I am totally convinced that simple approaches are the best way to make all of your players understand what you want from them. In football, as in life, the ones who can understand are the ones who dominate. I grew up playing a lot of street football, where the game gets played freely and improvements come naturally to people, without pushing. Then I became a manager who really believes in the essence of the game, and it's all from simplicity. If a coach tries to reinvent this logic, they are going in the wrong direction. I've been defending this philosophy for years.

Interview Felipe Rocha

THE DETAILS

The former Real Madrid flop's been a hit in Iran since taking over in 2011

Age
65

Birthplace
Mozambique

Current position
Iran head coach

Formation
4-3-3

Playing style
Counter-attack

Teams managed
9

World Cup qualifications
South Africa (2002)
Portugal (2010)
Iran (2014, 2018)

Biggest achievement
Leading Iran to two World Cups in a row

Lowest moment
Sacked by Real Madrid in 2004 after finishing 4th in La Liga

masterclass

DOMINIC CALVERT-LEWIN

Everton's quicksilver forward talks cage football, maturing out on loan and tips off Wayne Rooney

You're a Sheffield lad – what are your earliest football memories?
I grew up in Hillsborough near Sheffield Wednesday's stadium, but I'm a Blade. My family support United, so I grew up following them. I always went down to the local park as there was this concrete court where you could play football and basketball. I used to play on there with a group of mates against older players. We were pretty decent so we'd always give them a good game, but I remember a few times when I got smashed in the mouth by a flailing arm!

> "Rooney's been helping me a lot with some little pointers. It's the small things that end up making a big difference"

Do you think cage football can help to develop young players?
I played a lot of cage and street football and it definitely served me well. I would train on a Tuesday and a Thursday when I was a kid, and outside of that I'd be in the cage or at the park. A lot of talent is coming through the various age groups for England and many players have that street background, so I think it's helping to create skilful footballers.

How important is it for young players to have role models?
I always remember dreaming of playing for Sheffield United at Bramall Lane. I'd watched players such as Kyle Naughton, Kyle Walker and later on Harry Maguire coming through and that gave me a lot of hope. I was about 14 or 15 and trying to get a scholarship when Naughton and Walker were breaking through, so seeing them being given a chance was inspiring.

You were loaned out a couple of times before making your first Blades start. How did that aid your progress?
It helped me prepare mentally as much as anything else. I gradually got used to the pressure of playing in front of bigger crowds. You don't really experience it at academy level. I can remember coming on as a sub at Bramall Lane for the first time and playing against Chesterfield. It was a local derby and there was almost 30,000 fans there. I was scared of giving the ball away and making a mistake, as I was worried what people would think. Spending time out on loan helped me to get over all of that and just carry on with my normal game.

Did it force you to mature?
Definitely. I had a one-month loan spell with Stalybridge Celtic in the Conference North. I had a little car and would go up to a service station, then get on the bus to travel to matches with the lads. That was the first time I felt like I was part of a proper team. Thinking about it now, it was a crucial time for me because I was learning my craft. Playing on the type of pitches you often play on in non-league, scoring goals and having fans cheer for you properly was a very important stage of my development.

Is there a big gulf between the lower leagues and the Premier League?
Stalybridge had players who had been in academies and then played in Leagues One and Two, so there are good players at that level. But the style of football is different. We never played out from the back – we'd just boot the ball up the pitch, spin it in behind and chase it. The difference between League One and League Two is not that big. You'll get some teams that play football and some that are physical, and I think that's pretty much the same for both divisions. The Premier League is a different standard of football.

You joined Everton in 2016 - was that a huge step up in quality?
What first made me go 'Wow' were the possession drills in training, when you're just playing keep-ball. Nobody gave the ball away and it was pinging everywhere. Everyone played one- and two-touch, so I realised I had to know where my next pass was going before I'd even received it. You take your touch and then pass it off, and you think to yourself, 'Yes, I kept the ball!' It was a case of small steps for me. The quality and speed of the passing was incredible – the ball never really left the ground. It was a significant step up from the under-23s.

What have you picked up from playing alongside Wayne Rooney?
I was over the moon when I heard that he was coming back to the club because he's a well-decorated English footballer. I think I'd be lying if I didn't say I was in awe when he first came into training, as any youngster would be. His quality was there for everyone to see from the start. He has been helping me quite a lot with some little pointers. It's the small things that end up making the biggest difference – when you put them all together, you'll become a more rounded footballer. He's improved my positioning and my body shape as I receive the ball, which will make the game a lot easier for me. You need all the help you can get as a youngster in the Premier League, and Wayne has been a huge help to me so far.

THE DETAILS

The young Toffee has proven to be a valuable asset to his new manager

Age
21

Height
1.87m

Shirt number
29

Total appearances
77

Goals
15

Assists
8

Premier League goals
9

League Cup goals
5

Europa League goals
1

*Up to January 14, 2019

Interview Ben Welch

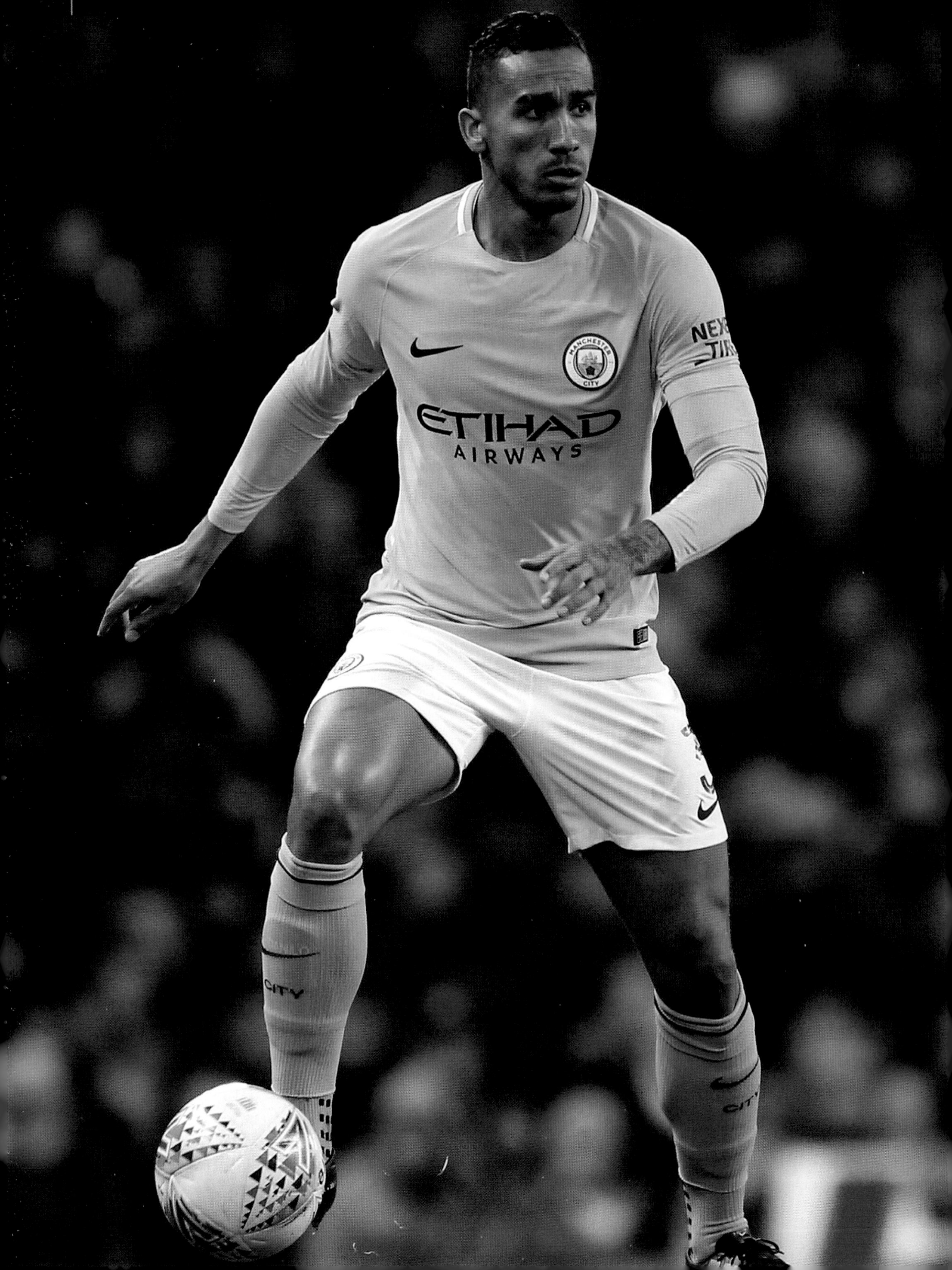
ETIHAD
AIRWAYS

masterclass

DANILO

The Brazilian talks Pep and playing out from the back

> "Most Brazilian full-backs start out as forwards, so they maintain that attacking spirit and have higher levels of technical skill"

So many dynamic, attacking full-backs have come from Brazil over the years. Why is that?

Well, Brazil sets the standard for most positions, right? But I think one of the secrets that explains why we produce quality full-backs is that a lot of them start out as forwards or midfielders, so perhaps have higher levels of technical skill. They still maintain that attacking spirit, and maybe have more creativity when it comes to taking on opponents. I think that's the big difference.

Which Brazilian players did you look up to as a youngster?

Like most full-backs, especially of my generation, Cafu was someone I looked up to a lot. Not only did he win almost every competition there was to win at Sao Paulo and Milan, he also lifted the World Cup with the national team and was an example of what it means to be a true leader on and off the pitch.

You've played as both a full-back and central midfielder – which is the more challenging role in terms of fitness?

Probably full-back. If you play there, it's important to have the explosiveness to sprint forward and support the attacks, but you also need enough stamina to go straight back to your defensive area. In central midfield it's a little different; the urgency isn't always as high but you have to be constantly on the move and adjusting your position all the time.

I enjoy both roles, though. Regardless of where I'm playing, I love football. In the last few seasons at Real Madrid and Manchester City I've played at full-back, but I'd still feel very comfortable in the middle of the pitch.

Modern widemen are often incredible athletes. Do you have to be in tip-top condition to become a flying full-back at the highest level?

Yes, definitely. Football is very dynamic these days and every player needs to be athletic. But the full-backs are usually among the players who run the furthest during matches, so you have to be well prepared and well rested. You need to treat your body properly, as you've got to preserve as much energy as possible. The importance of good rest and good sleep is something I've learnt down the years – I have to take care of my body because it's my tool.

What tips would you give to a young full-back to improve their game?

There's one key thing: whenever you go forward and have the chance to create an opportunity for a team-mate, make sure to get your head up and try to spot your target early. That applies to passes into the penalty area as well as crosses.

My other piece of advice would be to enjoy the role. In Brazil that's something we try to do wherever we play, but when you're a full-back and working so hard up and down the wing for 90 minutes, you have to really love your job.

You've played in La Liga and the Premier League – how does the intensity of the two divisions compare?

Both of them are really intense, but in different ways. In the Spanish league, most of the clubs aren't worried about defending or being completely solid at the back, so the games involving those teams are usually more open. A lot of attacking players in Spain are technical. There are so many South Americans there, but the Spanish players have that kind of style, too.

In the Premier League, attackers are fast and strong, but also clinical. If you give them just a little bit of space, they will use it to create a chance. You have to be focused for the whole game and there are never any breaks.

Pep Guardiola likes full-backs who are capable of playing in multiple positions. What individual instructions does he give you?

As incredible as this may seem, when it comes to bringing the ball out from the back and moving forward, he gives me a lot of freedom as he knows my strengths. He tells me to follow my instinct and use my experience.

Guardiola gives me more instructions about defending. I must help the team recover its shape, form that back line of four, and win the ball back as quickly as possible whenever we lose possession. He asks these things of every defender at the club, though.

Guardiola also likes his defenders to play the ball out from the back. How much training do you need to master this tactic under pressure?

Every week in training we'll do sessions in reduced spaces, under pressure from the other team, with restrictions on the number of touches we can take. Having done that repeatedly during the week in training, we then go out onto the bigger space of the pitch on a Saturday and it happens more easily. Of course, there are other kinds of pressure thrown into the mix when you're actually playing a match – the crowd, the importance of the game - but we're all players with strong personalities who've also played for our national teams and in huge matches. So what we practise in training should be enough to give us the confidence needed to play this way. For me, playing in that style – with very high possession and hundreds of passes – is incredibly fun. It's definitely the one I enjoy the most.

THE DETAILS

The versatile Samba star has enjoyed a trophy-laden career thus far

Full name
Danilo Luiz da Silva

Birthplace
Bicas, Brazil

Age
27

Clubs
America Mineiro, Santos, Porto, Real Madrid, Man City

Major honours
Copa Libertadores, La Liga, Champions League (x2), Premier League, League Cup

Club appearances
348

Club goals
31

International debut
2011 vs Argentina

International caps
22

Interview Felipe Rocha

«Up to January 13, 2019

Interview Steve Brenner

the defender

SAMI HYYPIA

The former Liverpool and Finland centre-back made more than 450 outings for the Reds and is his country's second most-capped player ever. He explains what it takes to forge an impenetrable defensive partnership

He may not have been a particularly high-profile signing when he joined Liverpool from Dutch side Willem II in 1999, but centre-back Sami Hyypia would soon establish himself as the defensive rock in a trophy-laden era for the Reds.

Former Liverpool chief scout Ron Yeats described the acquisition of the Finnish man-mountain as "one of the best bits of business we've done over the years. A steal, a bargain."

A two-time Finnish Cup winner with MyPa, he formed a formidable central defensive partnership with fellow new signing Stephane Henchoz, and in their second season the duo helped Gerard Houllier's outfit capture a League Cup, FA Cup and UEFA Cup treble.

Hyypia later paired up with England defender Jamie Carragher, an alliance that helped the Anfield giants, by now under the stewardship of Spanish boss Rafael Benitez, to win the Champions League in 2004-05.

You played in an era when the game was awash with sublime centre-backs. Do you think there's now a dearth of world-class defenders?

There's still the same quality today but when you look at modern centre-backs, most of them are very good on the ball, rather than physically strong. The game has evolved and now a lot of teams look to play out from the back and then build from there, so the centre-backs are an important part of the process. If they're unable to play with the ball at their feet, it's impossible to succeed.

It's difficult to compare players from different times. Maybe some defenders now wouldn't be able to cope with the game 15 years ago, and vice versa. The game seems to get quicker all the time: players are fitter and some teams play with a high line and like to press, so it's more demanding for the centre-backs. That means there's often space behind you, which can also cause problems.

Who are the best centre-backs in the modern game?
There are lots, but I still follow Liverpool closely and I've been so impressed with Virgil van Dijk since he joined in January. He's a big, strong centre-back, but also excellent in possession. It seemed like he took charge from day one, talking to his team-mates and giving instructions all the time, which is great to see.

You formed watertight partnerships with both Henchoz and Carragher at Anfield – what was the secret to your success alongside them?
Communication. You need at least one of the pair to be vocal during the game. With Henchoz I talked more than him, but with Carragher (above right) it was both of us. Myself and Stephane just clicked right away and understood each other immediately. From the first game we played together, it felt like we'd been a pairing for many years.

I arrived at the club at the same time as a few other foreign players, so we used to help each other out in the week and spoke a lot. That was important when it came to our partnership on the pitch. You also need to be comfortable enough to discuss what you both did wrong and what can be improved upon. There were some partnerships in my career where the communication wasn't there and that makes it difficult to work as a pairing. Together you are stronger.

You once went 87 games for Liverpool without getting booked - how did you manage that? As a centre-back, how important is it to keep your emotions in check for 90 minutes?
A few managers in my career actually encouraged me to be a bit nastier, but I was a naturally calm guy on the field. Once or twice the red mist descended, but most of the time I was able to keep my cool. Perhaps some of my 50/50 challenges hurt the opposition, but I always tried to be fair.

You played against so many quality centre-forwards in your career. Which style of opponent did you find most difficult to deal with, and who was the best forward you ever faced?
Little, nippy strikers were the most challenging to play against. I wasn't the fastest, which meant they were the most difficult ones to stop.

I often get asked which was the best forward I ever faced. There were loads of incredible strikers in that era, but I'd have to choose Thierry Henry - he had speed, technique... everything! He was always tough to play against whenever we played Arsenal. With him, it wasn't the physical battle I was worried about.

You've admitted you weren't blessed with blistering speed, so how did you ensure you weren't exposed by pacy forwards? Is positioning key to this?
From a young age I knew I wasn't the quickest defender in the world, so I'd have to

"A few managers encouraged me to be nastier, but I was a naturally calm guy on the pitch – I tried to lead by example"

be mentally ready for a battle with my opponent or I'd really struggle. You need to think about how close you should be to the forward when he gets the ball. For me, if I was marking a fast striker and he stepped towards the ball, I wouldn't let him turn and run towards me and the goal - I'd want to win the ball back straight away.

You won trophies under Houllier and Benitez at Liverpool - did they expect different things from their defenders?
They didn't necessarily expect different things, but there were small differences when it came to their approaches. Rafa was very much about the details - he'd analyse so many videos and if he saw even something really minor, he'd want us to work on it.

I remember the morning after a game we'd won 3-0. I went to training feeling good, but then we had a video meeting and the footage was all of the negative moments from the night before! He was always trying to be better. It helped me though, and I learned so much. Gerard wasn't quite so analytical, but he had his own strengths and kept the atmosphere in the squad very positive.

You captained Liverpool - how would you describe your leadership style and how did you inspire your team-mates?
I always tried to lead by example, both in training sessions and out on the pitch. I gave 100% and wanted to improve - it was important the other players saw that. I wasn't a shouter in the changing room, but Houllier wouldn't have made me captain if he hadn't appreciated my other qualities. He never wanted me to change. I tried to be a positive influence and encourage players - shouting until I was red in the face wasn't my style.

EIDUR GUDJOHNSEN

The former Chelsea and Barcelona striker on how being versatile earlier in his career helped him to excel at the highest level

Interview Chris Flanagan

Only one Icelander has ever tasted Champions League glory, and Eidur Gudjohnsen's rise to the top owed as much to intelligence as it did to speed or physique.

Like Teddy Sheringham before him, Gudjohnsen made the 'second striker' role his own, combining anticipation with technique to claim two Premier League titles at Chelsea and become a European champion with Barcelona.

He tells *FFT* how he did it...

Which players did you admire when you were a child?

I watched my father a lot – he played in an Anderlecht team that challenged for European Cups. He made this video of the goals he'd scored and I used to watch it all the time. The main things I learned from him were his drive and his character to never stop. Then I had the privilege of him teaching me a few things. The key one was to anticipate the game and what may happen next.

You were an intelligent player who found space with clever movement. Who influenced your style?

Dick Advocaat was my coach at PSV Eindhoven, the one who took me into the first-team squad before I was 17. He taught me how to create space for myself. Don't stand still, and always be on the move – it doesn't have to be a sprint. Anticipate where the ball may drop and learn to play off your team-mates. I was lucky to play with players like Jan Wouters, who was in the Holland team that won Euro 88.

If you were coaching a young player with a similar style to yourself, what tips would you give them?

Know how all of your team-mates play. By doing that, you understand how they want to release the ball, and whether they want to play it off you or find you in between the lines. Lose your marker by making short moves in the opposite direction to drag them a yard away from you. It makes it harder for the defender to anticipate what you want to do.

What was the best piece of advice you ever received from a team-mate?

Be more selfish. That was in my younger years, when I was more of a No.9. Don't be happy with scoring one goal; get two and three. I never ended up doing that, but it was good advice. That was from Wouters – he said, 'If you stand still for two seconds, I'll kick the

"In Holland the forwards took care of finishing, but in England Big Sam made me realise that defending starts from the front"

absolute s**t out of you!' [*Laughs*]

What was the most important lesson you learned as a striker?
After missing a chance, there'll always be the next one to make up for it. After every game, use the next game to make up for the mistakes you've made. A bad display or bad miss can keep you awake. When I was 17, I came off the bench for PSV against Barcelona in the UEFA Cup and missed two great chances. Then in the 80th minute, Sergi scored to knock us out - it kept me awake for a month. If you find the capacity to forget misses like that and focus on the next match, things will get easier. Don't dwell on it.

How did you hone your link-up play?
Although I started as a No.9, I played as both an attacking midfielder and sitting midfielder when the team had injuries. Advocaat was aware I had the capacity to play in different areas, because of the way I read the game and the fact that my close control was good. I knew how to control a ball, fend off defenders and bring others into play. By playing several roles you get a bigger view of the pitch.

Did you do drills with specific players that you'd be partnering?
This was a different era when there'd be two strikers most of the time, so you'd find the player you played upfront with and do drills linking up with them. There would also be drills anticipating what to do when the ball's on the wing - moving off each other into the penalty area - so you're not occupying the same spaces.

Would you stay behind after training?
I would, but not for long as I broke my leg when I was younger so was always afraid to overtrain. I felt my limits and knew when I'd done enough. I'd maybe go for a run in the evening instead. You can always do more, but you have to be careful not to go over the limit, as that's when injury risks come in.

What advice would you give to a striker about staying cool in front of goal?
Don't have the fear of missing. That's the biggest problem that can creep into a footballer's confidence. Don't be afraid to make a mistake - just go and score with your next chance.

Which was your preferred position?
Attacking midfield or playing off a main striker - that's where I helped the team the most. My freedom depended on the manager. In Holland the two frontmen took care of finishing the attacks. When I went to England, especially under Sam Allardyce at Bolton, I soon realised that we're not only forwards - the defending starts earlier than seeing an opponent sprint past you and just standing there.

How did your positioning alter when the team were in or out of possession?
It'd be influenced by how we planned to defend as a team. At Chelsea, there would be games where Jose Mourinho told me to push up as a second striker if we weren't winning and try to influence things going forward. But as soon as we went ahead, he'd say, 'Now become the third midfielder and we can overcrowd them.'
Sometimes you'll pick up a position ready to go on the counter-attack as you think, 'They're not going to cause us any trouble'. That's a risk you take by reading the game.

masterclass

PAUL SCHOLES

The Manchester United midfield legend on pinging passes and breaking the net

Paul, you were one of the best passers of a football we've ever seen – what was your secret?

Passing was something that came naturally to me. Until the age of 18 I was a striker, but [former Manchester United youth team coach] Eric Harrison always thought I would be a central midfielder. He saw something in my passing and felt I could be a creative player. I was lucky at United, because Alex Ferguson would constantly tell me to play the ball forwards. When I had time on the ball, my first thought was always to look for my two wide players and my two strikers. The last resort was a sideways or backwards pass.

> "I always looked forward when I had time on the ball. Passing it sideways or backwards was the last resort"

Did you adjust your passing style for different types of strikers?

Absolutely. I knew Andy Cole would always be on the shoulder of the last man. I didn't even have to say anything; it would just take a bit of eye contact and then I'd play a through-ball or hit a pass over the top. Ruud van Nistelrooy was very similar to Cole in that sense: I could dink it over the top and he'd be away. But then you have players such as Teddy Sheringham and Dwight Yorke who were No.10s, really – they were the players who could play one-twos and little passes around the corner. I would link up with them first and then look to find the second centre-forward.

How important is courage on the ball if you want to dictate play?

It's huge. The big reason I retired the first time, in 2011, was because I felt that I had lost a lot of my bottle. If you don't have bottle, you won't play for Manchester United. You have to have the balls to play and get on the ball. I was playing safe passes and keeping everything nice and easy. I wasn't having any real benefit on the team because I wasn't doing the things I did earlier in my career. I'd stopped taking risks. Players such as Toni Kroos, Luka Modric and Andrea Pirlo have the bottle to get on the ball and then control the tempo of a game from start to finish.

You ended your career as a holding midfielder. How did you adapt?

I don't normally like that term because I think as a midfielder you should be able to do everything. But positioning is really important in that role. Rio Ferdinand didn't like me dropping too deep to pick up the ball. He'd say to me, 'Go away, get out of my space'. Communication with the two central defenders is crucial – they're the ones pulling you about and telling you where they want you. If they do that well, they make everything easy for you.

You played as a No.10 for a season as well. What's the difference between this role and playing in midfield?

When you're further forward, you have to be able to receive the ball in different positions and have the awareness to play with your back to goal. I was lucky that I played with Ruud van Nistelrooy: he was a great centre-forward, great at link-up play, and I loved playing with him. I was never fast – though I was OK over five yards – but when I was younger I had the sharpness to play that role. As I got older, I didn't feel as comfortable playing in that position. I'd start to struggle if I found myself in a one-on-one situation with a defender because I wasn't that great a dribbler. I preferred to play a one-two with someone and beat a man that way.

So you weren't blessed with great pace as a footballer, and yet you were rarely caught in possession. Why do you think this was?

I think it was my awareness. Eric Harrison would hammer that home. He told me to have a glance over my shoulder even if the ball was 50 yards away. He said a central midfield player should always know where he is on a football pitch and have a picture in his mind of where everyone else is. If you do this, you know where your next pass is before you even get the ball. When I picked up the ball on the left wing, I knew David Beckham was wide on the right, and without looking I could turn and hit the ball over there. I was never a great runner or a great athlete, but my brain was always sharp.

A lot of your goals came through powerful shots rather than carefully placed finishes. Why was that?

A lot of my finishing came down to instinct – I don't think I was a very good finisher when I had plenty of time to think about a shot. I would always go for power. Whether it was a header or a shot from the edge of the box, I'd put my foot through it and hope that it went in the right direction. Sometimes there would be a bit of guile behind it, but I would rarely attempt a sidefoot finish. It just wasn't something I was good at doing.

Interview Alec Fenn

THE DETAILS

Scholes by numbers

41
Age

168
Height in centimetres (around 5ft 6in)

1994
Year of debut

18
Squad number at Manchester United

66
England caps

14
England goals

90%
Pass completion in 2010-11 Premier League season

11
Premier League titles

2
Champions League winner's medals

3
FA Cup crowns

masterclass

THEO WALCOTT

The speed demon explains the secret training sessions he uses that have supercharged his game

> "Last season, I tried to pick on Harry Maguire who is about twice my size, so I don't mind getting stuck in"

Hi Theo. How vital is extra training to staying fit and fast for a full season?

I think it's important to always stay one step ahead of everyone else. If you can find a way to improve your game by one per cent, then you are going to have an advantage over your opponent. As you get older you need to take care of your body, as you can feel the intensity of the Premier League improving after every season. The younger players are all physically able to compete and that makes it even more competitive for a place in the team. You have to make sure you're always fit and ready to go.

Players often post images of their workout sessions on social media – does that provide competition?

I'm someone who isn't too bothered about what other people are doing. I'm good at just focusing on myself and making sure that I do the little things right. If you are professional and do everything properly on the training field, in the gym and outside of the club, things will fall in place. I like to have my week planned out, so I know when I head into a game I haven't cut any corners. But there is definitely a bit of competition when you see the other players doing workouts on social media – sometimes you will see a coach using one of your drills. It's all fun and games.

Do you include any additional sprint work in your daily training routines?

After I'd ruptured my anterior cruciate ligament [against Spurs in 2014] I was introduced to a sprint coach. I felt that was the first thing I needed to look at. Speed is a huge part of my game – I'm never going to be an endurance runner – and I was keen to make sure I didn't lose my pace. I often do footwork drills with ladders or reaction sessions using cones to retain sharpness. When I was young I tried to do 100-metre running at county level, but my technique was nowhere near that of trained sprinters. I never really got the chance to work on it, but who knows – maybe I would have been a sprinter if I'd carried on with it?

You turned 28 in March having agreed to join Arsenal at 16. Have you had to modify training as you've got older?

I have always done quite a lot of work away from the training ground, so I'm continuing to do all of the right things. I've worked with a personal trainer on my core strength, because I've always believed that was a weakness of mine. I also spend some time in cryotherapy chambers and ice baths, while various stretching exercises help me to recover from training sessions and matches as quickly as possible. They definitely help because I very rarely have aching legs afterwards, so I'm capable of playing in a game once every two or three days.

With a couple of young kids at home now, is your recovery regime affected?

Not too much. I'm quite lucky because normally they sleep through the night and wake up at about 5.30am. I get up with them and once I'm up, I'm up, so I don't go back to bed or anything like that. Once I'm in my car and heading off for training, my focus is all on that, and then when I go back home again I'm a dad. Having kids is really good; they're a healthy distraction from football and it means I can switch off from the game.

Do you think you need a nasty streak to play at the highest level nowadays?

Yes and no. I'm the type of person who will be aggressive when I need to be – and that's when I play my best football. Last season, I tried to pick on Hull City defender Harry Maguire who is twice my size, so I don't mind getting stuck in. I'll take my fair share of kicks but always get straight back up again. The opposition hate that as they know they can't affect you mentally. I like to use my body more on the pitch these days, because I feel stronger physically.

Footballers can get plenty of stick on social media – how important is it to block it out and be mentally strong?

That's just the way the world is today. People like to comment on everything but, to be honest, I don't really see any of it. One of the most important things is to listen to all of the people around you, such as family, your coaches and your own thoughts, too. I do what I do for me. I don't worry about opinions of others who know nothing about me.

You have played as both a striker and wideman for Arsenal - have modern players got to be tactically versatile?

I think so, yes. Around 10-15 years ago everybody in England played in a 4-4-2 formation. However, now there is more variety, which means you've got to be able to adapt. When I first started out with Southampton I was a forward in a 4-4-2 system. I learned a lot from watching people like Michael Owen and Emile Heskey – they had a great big man, little man partnership at Liverpool. I have played in quite a few positions since I joined Arsenal, but I think the right wing is where I will feature the most this season.

masterclass

JAMAAL LASCELLES

The Newcastle stopper is the youngest skipper in the Premier League – he reveals how he leads his troops

You're the Premier League's youngest captain – was it a surprise to be given the armband so soon?

It's a massive achievement. I thought it would be a big task in terms of pressure and the expectation of the role, because Newcastle's fans demand the best. But the backing of Rafa Benitez and advice from all of the coaching staff has helped me to adapt quickly.

Has it been a challenge giving orders to players with a lot more experience?

Probably more so in the 2016-17 season as we had more experienced players at the club. Last season the average age of the squad came down, so quite a lot of the lads were a similar age to myself or a couple of years older. I think I'm a big character in the dressing room, though, so I'm comfortable with it.

It would have been more difficult had I become the captain immediately after I signed, but I've been at Newcastle for a few years now and that's been a huge help. I know everyone and there's a level of respect there already.

Did you captain teams when you were an academy player?

Yeah. I've always liked being the leader of a team and enjoyed the responsibility. Whenever I played at primary school or secondary school, I was always captain. When I joined Nottingham Forest, I was their captain at under-16, under-18 and reserve-team level. I think the only time I haven't been captain is at youth-team level for England and when I first arrived at Newcastle in 2014.

Do you think the game is producing as many leaders as it used to?

The type of player coming through the academies has changed, as managers prefer ball-players and technicians. But sometimes that means you don't have big personalities in the dressing room or that old-school mentality.

I think my attributes are pretty rare in the modern game. If you look at a lot of the bigger clubs, they're not as vocal as they used to be, and there aren't players like Tony Adams, Steven Gerrard or John Terry captaining teams any more.

How would you describe your style of communication? Do you ever have to scream and shout?

It took me a little while to understand how to get my message across to some of the squad. Rafa has sat me down on a few occasions and explained I can't communicate the same way with every player. It's up to me how I learn to talk to them, and over time I've worked out which guys can handle me yelling and which like an arm around the shoulder.

I reckon I've definitely improved that part of my game. I've also been helped by the fact we've kept the same group of players together, so I've got to know them all individually.

What has Benitez (below) taught you since he arrived as manager in 2016?

He's always correcting small things with me and talking to me. He will tell me to watch clips of various players to improve my game. He's by far the best manager I've worked with – he's very easy to talk to and his door is always open.

You can tell he's managed at the highest level, and every day it's like playing in front of a new manager because he has authority and commands respect immediately. Players want to impress him in training because of his stature and what he's achieved during his career.

He's known as a master tactician, so has he helped you tactically?

Yeah, he's big on tactics – not so much skill and technique but positioning, and controlling the back line and the spaces between defence and midfield. Anyone who watched Newcastle last season will have noticed we're pretty hard to break down, and that's all down to his tactics. He's such a perfectionist. If it's not right, he'll stop training and correct us.

Steven Gerrard once said it was hard to earn Benitez's praise at Liverpool. Do you struggle to get the Spaniard's nod of approval?

Some managers will just praise you all the time, but even if you do something well at Newcastle, Rafa will tell you how you can do it even better. It's rare that he praises players, as he knows no one here is potentially where they should be in terms of the level they can take this team to. He knows I've got a long way to go. I'm only 24, so rather than praise me, he'll give me advice.

Which centre-backs did you look up to when you were younger?

When I was 16 I was training with the first-team squad at Nottingham Forest. Wes Morgan was the main centre-back and my role model. I loved the way he defended: Wes was so dominant in the air and loved putting his foot in. It's no surprise that he's had big success with Leicester and won the Premier League.

Have you changed as a player since making the step up to the top flight?

In the Championship I was a lot bigger physically, but I've trimmed down and worked hard on speed and agility. When you're coming up against players like Raheem Sterling and Sergio Aguero, you have to make sure you're as fast as possible and be able to change direction quickly.

Lascelles was speaking to EA Sports, an official partner of the Premier League.

> "My attributes are rare in the modern game. Managers prefer ball-players and you have fewer big personalities coming through"

Interview Alec Fenn

THE DETAILS

The Magpie's won almost 60 per cent of his tackles in the top tier

Age
24

Premier League appearances
51

Clean sheets
12

Tackles
43

Tackle success
58%

Interceptions
56

Clearances
307

Aerial battles won
170

Successful 50/50s
8

*Up to the end of 2017-18 campaign

PATRICK VIEIRA

Nice's new gaffer on the challenge of making the transition from player to coach, and how he would manage his younger self

Interview Martin Harasimowicz

Great footballers don't always make great managers, but France's 1998 World Cup-winning side continue to buck that trend.

Zinedine Zidane – who scored twice in the 1998 showpiece – captured his third consecutive Champions League crown as Real Madrid supremo in May, before Didier Deschamps became only the third person to win the World Cup as a player and manager a couple of months later.

Laurent Blanc has also enjoyed his fair share of success on the sidelines, guiding both Paris Saint-Germain and Bordeaux to the Ligue 1 title.

So it's easy to see why Patrick Vieira could follow in his fellow countrymen's footsteps. The 42-year-old ex-Arsenal and Inter midfielder was named Nice coach in June, after spells in charge of Manchester City's elite development squad and New York City FC. He chats to *FFT* about completing the transition from player to gaffer...

Has your playing background helped you as a coach?

In some situations, definitely. I think being a former player has helped me to anticipate what other players are feeling. Now I try to anticipate issues within the squad before they arise, or develop from being a minor problem into something more serious.

My experience as a player has really helped me to understand how players form a bond inside the dressing room. It allows me to predict a lot of things, even on the field.

Do you need to have played the game to be a top coach?

I think if you've been a player, it makes the transition to becoming a manager that little bit easier. You can anticipate what could be going through a player's mind, but that isn't the decisive factor behind whether you'll be a good coach or a bad coach.

If you've been a player, you'll win the dressing room for about the first three months because it gives you credibility. However, that doesn't last forever and beyond that it's all about the philosophy and message you send to your players. That makes the difference.

Does coaching bring similar rewards compared to playing?

As a coach, I'm still a part of the game we all love so much, although it's more frustrating than being a player. You can prepare for the game; you can give the information to the squad; you can have your gameplan finalised; you can be so well prepared. But you have no control once the game kicks off, and that's the really annoying thing.

On the field you're the actor and you can control what's happening. If you're sat on the bench it's hard. Sometimes I would love to lace up my boots again and take care of everything, but I can't do that any more!

"If you've been a player, you'll win the dressing room for three months as you have credibility — then it's all about your philosophy"

What's the most challenging aspect of coaching?

It's the change of mindset you have to make, having been a player your whole life. As a player, all you ever think about is yourself, but as a coach you must be unselfish and consider everyone else. You need great personal skills to show empathy and understand the different individuals with different personalities.

This is something I needed to change quickly in the first few months. I think it's key for a coach to have a consistent mood whether you're winning or losing. It's important to conduct yourself the same way around the training ground and around the players, because that breeds trust. If a player doesn't know how you behave on a day-to-day basis, that can harm your relationship.

How do you like to communicate with your players?

Communication is essential. If you can't do it well then you'll never become a top coach. I try to strike a balance between speaking to players individually, so they know specifically what I want, and also speaking to them collectively, so they'll understand team objectives. I believe in making it as simple as possible to help them perform. Giving players too many instructions can confuse them and then hamper their decision-making.

How would you describe your football philosophy?

I think it's important for my team to play a style of football I enjoy watching. I always want my team to score goals, but what I really want from the players is for them to go onto the pitch and try to win in a positive way. I want them to go forward, play positive football and take risks, and I want to see goals. When the team is scoring a lot of goals, the players enjoy themselves and fans get value for money.

Are you someone who studies a lot or speaks to other coaches and leaders?

I was very lucky to play under some of the world's best managers and I took something from each of them, as they were all different but all had success. I can't try to pretend to be one of them, though. That would be a huge mistake. If I did that, I wouldn't be me and the players would see through it.

I must be clear about my philosophy and the way I want my team to play. It is key for me to understand who I want to be as a coach and stick to that style.

How would you coach a young Patrick Vieira if you came across him today?

I'd give him more precise formations to express his talent, and also more specific details about what I want and don't want from him. I was a player who thrived on individual communications and the little details from the coach. I never wanted to go onto the pitch with an empty page. I needed to know the manager had a specific purpose for me in the match.

JAVI MARTINEZ

Bayern Munich's versatile defender on the art of dominating play as the pivot

Describe the Javi Martinez way.

The ball is, and always will be, my friend. I need to touch the ball and I suffer if I don't have it. When the opposition have got the ball, then it is my job – whether I'm playing as a central defender or a defensive midfielder – to fight to win the ball back in one-on-one situations. My role is a defensive one, to help my team-mates all of the time and to give them what they want: the ball.

What drills should a youngster be practising to dominate a match while playing in the pivot role?

Above all else, your positioning is so important – it is almost an art form. Putting yourself in the right place, in an attacking and more defensive sense, to receive the ball is crucial. Drills that teach a young player how to anticipate controlling the ball on the half-turn, so they can 'roll out' to the next man and keep the move going, are fundamental. But there's more. You must also learn about the first pass and the long ball to switch the direction of attack. Always think: 'How can my next pass hurt the other team the most or help my own team?'

You have played a lot of games as both centre-back and defensive midfielder. How do the physical demands of the two different positions compare?

They are very similar, especially under Pep Guardiola at Bayern Munich. He always wanted me to play as a third central midfielder and to move up to help the attack and dominate the ball. Under Carlo Ancelotti it is now a little different, as there's a slightly greater emphasis on defending. But my role is still to use my physique and get upfield. I've always said that I'll play where the team needs me. That will never change.

And tactically, how do they vary?

At the start, playing as a centre-back was really tough. I had played there under Marcelo Bielsa with Athletic Bilbao, but that was man-to-man marking so switching to zonal under Guardiola was difficult. It took hours and hours of hard work in training to really understand when to press the ball and to change your outlook, but in the end it's become second nature. Now I feel very comfortable there – it proves what hard work can achieve.

> "The ball is, and always will be, my friend. I need to touch the ball and I suffer if I don't have it"

How would you explain your style of play to a Martian if aliens landed?

[*Laughs*] That I'm the team's helper. That I can do that role either for an individual who needs support or for the team as a whole by organising players positionally. That I always give my maximum in every moment.

You've suffered a couple of serious injuries in recent years - mentally, how difficult is it to deal with an extended layoff on the sidelines?

You have to be very patient. You have to watch your team-mates train and play, but eventually you come back to doing what you love. Once you're able, you have to train to the maximum your body allows you. I'm strong mentally, so I was able to recover.

The use of rondos by Spanish clubs has become famous in recent years. How do they improve you as a player?

They teach you the fundamentals of the possession game – how to pass the ball, when to do so and where to position yourself in order to give your team-mates the best possible angle to pass you the ball. They're good fun, too – it's like you're not learning at all.

Who gets the lads going in the Bayern Munich dressing room?

There are a few guys in the dressing room who get us all fired up before the matches, but Rafinha is always joking before kick-off and getting us ready to go out and play. He's a great guy, one of my best mates in football.

With today's round-the-clock sports coverage, is it possible for a modern player to relax away from the pitch?

Definitely, I think it's really important. I like playing on the PlayStation. I love the cinema and doing new things. This season I'm going to do a long-distance learning course with a university back home in Spain, as I did not like leaving my studies behind. I have always been interested in journalism, so I'm going to get involved in that and see how it goes. Who knows, it could possibly be something to do after I finish football?

You're the youngest of four siblings - how did your upbringing as a child influence your career as a footballer?

Hugely. I would always attempt to copy my brother from an early age. He's nine years older than I am. I was always trying to play with him and all of his friends around our village and I'd usually follow him to games when he played for the Athletic Club second team – I owe my brother a great deal and he has always been a reference point for me.

THE DETAILS

The history buff reveals his heroes & hoop dreams

Childhood hero
My brother, Alvaro

Superstition
Visualising the game

Favourite sport - other than football
I'm a basketball fan

Dream Bayern Munich signing
Nobody! We've got the perfect squad

Favourite flick
Untouchable – it is a French film

Favourite music
I like listening to Ryan Adams a lot

Dream coffee date
The New York Knicks' Derrick Rose (above)

If you hadn't made it as a footballer...
I would have been a basketball player

Best friend
There's too many in football to mention

Best school subject - aside from sport
I was good at history

Interview Andrew Murray

masterclass

TROY DEENEY

The Watford captain explains how training sessions with Anthony Joshua's coach help him stay in shape

Do you reckon you can become a Premier League player without being an elite-level athlete?
No. I think you have to be technically very good, but now you're starting to see the emergence of a lot of players in the lower leagues who are willing to put the hard yards in. You look at people like Jamie Vardy, Andre Gray and myself: we've adapted to Premier League football because we've always been willing to put the extra physical work in. Lower down the leagues you have to just run for every ball, so that is why we've gone on to do very well.

You've done some work with Anthony Joshua's trainer, Jamie Reynolds, so how did that partnership come about?
I was one of the first players he worked with. About six years ago I saw a friend of mine training with him and thought, 'That's a bit different.' I'm always open to trying new things to develop myself physically, and the training that we do is high-intensity and tailored specifically to my game. Jamie was the first trainer who explained what physical attributes I needed as a striker, my strengths and weaknesses, and then he said, "I want to keep working at your strengths." I'd never worked with anybody specifically on my game before – previously I had only done training programmes which had been developed for a whole squad of players, rather than personal ones.

How often do you work with him?
I'll do a two- or three-week camp with Jamie before I go back to Watford for the start of pre-season. I will do lots of footwork and agility sessions so I have that sharpness. Rather than catching up during pre-season, I'll already be ahead. We also do some work together during the season but we tailor it to how many matches I have. It's not like a boxer who has a 12-week camp and knows exactly when they can train every week. If you have three games per week, it's almost impossible for you to do strength and conditioning work. Any big heavy lifting just fatigues the body when you need to be recovering for your next match.

You're good friends with Joshua – do you think there are many similarities between boxing and football fitness?
No, they're completely different. I watch a lot of boxing and will do some boxing training myself. I find that boxing is a lot more emotional – if you get punched in the face, your natural reaction is to get angry and react, but you can't do that. You just have to keep everything under control. Under the lights, it's incredibly hot as well – even when you're ringside you are sweating loads. As well as the environment being different, the boxers also use a completely different energy system. We will play on a Saturday and Tuesday for about 11 months, whereas they train for 12 weeks to get ready for a fight on a Saturday night. They have a three-month training camp for one fight and they do that maybe three times a year. Our bodies are put through more pain, I would say.

Do you need a lean physique to perform so many sprints during a single match?
Funnily enough, I've always been called bulky by away fans. They will phrase it slightly different to that, but they always suggest that I'm a big lad. However, you can't be the team captain and set an example if you are not fit. The lads wouldn't stand for it and the manager most definitely wouldn't. It's probably twice as hard for me to avoid putting on weight, because as soon as I put on a couple of pounds everybody can see it, so I have got to keep on top of it for the whole season.

Have you felt the impact of your gym work when you are out on the pitch?
The strength work I've done has helped to give me a mental edge, as I think I'm bigger and stronger than everyone else. The specific stuff I have done with Jamie has paid off with a few of the goals I've scored. The one against Southampton in March was a perfect example: the ball just bobbled up and I reacted to it really quickly and lifted it into the top corner. The reactive work I've done with Jamie has really helped me with goals like that.

What does your daily diet look like?
It is pretty colourful and varied – I have a friend who has set up a food company who are supplying Joshua and several Premier League footballers, and I'll use his products too. I eat a good variety of quality protein – one day it's steak, the next is chicken, then it'll be mincemeat. It all gets packed up for me, ready to go. I'll have around 50-100g of protein with lots of different fruit and vegetables and then about 25g of sweet potato as well.

> "The strength work has given me a mental edge – I think I'm bigger and stronger than everyone else"

THE DETAILS

The bricklayer from Brum's come a long way since his Walsall days

Age
30

Height
6ft

Childhood club
I'm a Brummie, so Birmingham City.

First professional football contract
£425.50 a week at Walsall. I still keep a picture of the pay slip on my phone.

Career highlight
Getting promoted at Watford – I was meant to leave the club that season...

Lowest moment
Serving three months in prison in 2012.

Premier League appearances
123

Premier League goals
33

*Up to January 14, 2019

Interview Alec Fenn

FRANK LAMPARD

The Chelsea legend on how lung-busting runs in the off-season turned him into a box-to-box star

Is there such thing as an off-season for a Premier League player?
I think the off-season is important for a Premier League player, but for me it didn't mean I put my feet up. Typically I had three or four weeks off during the summer and would balance that with pure relaxation, where I'd put the ball away to give my mind and body a full rest. After that, I'd spend a few weeks working my way up, ready for the start of pre-season training. It's important you don't spend too long not moving – you've got to look after your body and ensure you're prepared for pre-season. If you're playing catch-up you will get found out, as everything is monitored these days. The data will show if you are behind physically.

Did you adapt your diet during those two weeks of rest?
I was always very conscious of my diet when I was resting. It's easy to control your diet when you're in the routine of training at a club or playing at a major tournament, because all the food and drink is provided. Whenever I went on holiday, I gave myself freedom to enjoy the foods I might not be allowed to eat during the season. It helps you to relax, but you have to stay on top of your diet. If you afford yourself some leeway, you can't take it too far.

> "I'd always ask for the pass into my feet to be hard to control. I didn't like clean passes; I wanted to put myself under pressure"

As you got older, were there elements of pre-season which became harder?
It definitely got tougher. I was always a player who enjoyed pre-season, and I liked running and pushing my body to its limit. Pre-season is always difficult, and it needs to be to give you that base fitness before the season starts. In the latter years of my career, the recovery was harder. I had to make sure I didn't overdo it and looked at ways to recover quicker, like sleeping better, stretching more often and using ice baths.

Did you do any specific sessions which gave you a physical edge on the pitch?
From a very young age, I became aware that I needed to do extra work to get to the level I wanted to be at. I did a lot of running as I wanted to be a box-to-box midfielder, so I'd do box-to-box sprints

once or twice a week, in groups of eight to 10 runs, to replicate the demands of a match. I would literally run from the 18-yard box at one end of the pitch to the other, at 75-80 per cent of my top speed with brief recovery times, to put myself under pressure.

I'd then mix it up with shorter sprints for speed, endurance and power. I'd do shuttle runs – forwards, backwards and sideways – to replicate a game situation, and work on my agility and speed from a standing start. I used to do six to eight sets over different distances, which I felt would be similar to what I'd be doing in central midfield. I felt if I did that work, it put me ahead of my competitors in terms of pure fitness.

How long were your rest periods between those runs?
I was quite old school – I wasn't on the clock as such. If I did a box-to-box run, my walk back to the other penalty area would be the rest period, which I think took about 12-15 seconds. The run lasted a similar amount of time, so the work and rest periods were about 50-50. The rest wasn't very long because I wanted to keep putting myself under pressure, as you have to replicate the intensity of a game. All of the sprint work would be done over a distance no bigger than the 18-yard box. I'd sprint from the penalty spot to one corner and back, and then repeat that for the other three corners. That was one set, and then I'd rest for a short period before repeating the drill six to eight times.

Your goalscoring record was as good as some of the best strikers – how did you hone your finishing?
I worked incredibly hard on my finishing throughout my career. As a youngster, I decided that I didn't want to become a run-of-the-mill midfielder who could just stay central and affect possession, but not affect a game in terms of goals. I knew I needed to train hard to hone the technique. I worked on my arrival into the 18-yard box, and the timing of those runs. I did that by watching my other team-mates and seeing exactly where they liked to cross the ball from – or if it was a striker, where they liked to hold the ball up. So much of that was mental, repetitive work. In terms of my shooting, I tried to practise every type of finish I could imagine. I worked on long shots from distance and instinctive finishes inside the box, and I'd always ask for the pass into my feet to be hard to control, so that I'd be ready during a game. I didn't like clean passes; I wanted to put myself under pressure. I worked on six-yard box finishing a lot. I didn't think people would expect a central midfielder to pick up those positions, and I wanted to get into those areas.

Lampard was speaking on behalf of BBC Sport

THE DETAILS

Lamps lifted three Premier League titles and averaged a goal every 3.5 matches

Birthplace
Romford

Premier League appearances
609

Goals
177

Right foot
78

Left foot
12

Headers
13

Penalties
32

Free-kicks
5

Assists
102

Player of the Season
2004-05

England caps
106

England goals
29

Interview Ben Welch

MANOLO GABBIADINI

The Italian striker explains how to stay calm in front of goal and cope with high-pressure games

Hi Manolo. Are natural goalscorers just born or can they be developed?

Certain talents, in my opinion, you just have within you. However, training can help you improve certain skills and you should always train as hard as you can. It's important to work on every part of your game: right foot, left foot, heading the ball, protecting the ball, everything. You must always give 100 per cent to ensure you reach maximum potential. If your 100 per cent is a 6/10 in terms of quality, that's OK. If it's 4/10, that is OK as well. The important thing is that if you're capable of giving 4/10 in every game, you give 4/10, not 2/10. Then if you're talented enough to reach 10/10, you'd better reach 10/10, not 7/10. That is my objective – my right foot might be a 4/10, but the important thing is that I hit that 4/10 and never settle for 2/10. You have to practice with that mindset.

> "When Mihajlovic was Sampdoria manager he liked having free-kick competitions in training. He's still fantastic at them"

You got to play under free-kick master Sinisa Mihajlovic during your time at Sampdoria. Did he help you to see the game from a defender's point of view?

To be honest, he liked taking part in the free-kick competitions at the end of our training sessions, so he was offensive in his thinking. He's still fantastic at taking free-kicks, so it was great to have a boss who retained that enjoyment of playing.

Do you see similarities between your own style and that of other strikers?

No. I say that because I'm not a fan of comparisons. I think it's a little bit ugly to compare yourself to another player. However, one thing that people have always said – although I never really saw him play because I was little - is that I play a bit like the former Cagliari striker Gigi Riva. But other people have said it; I don't say it as I never got to see him in action. I know he was an incredible player, though, so that's nice to hear.

Do you think the role of the striker has changed much in recent years?

I believe the modern striker now has to be capable of doing everything. It isn't enough to just score goals. We are now expected to be the first line of defence, provide assists and stick the ball in the back of the net as well. And we have to be able to do all of those things in many formations, too. The more rounded you are as a player, the greater chance you will have of enjoying a successful career.

Lots of players lose their nerve in front of goal – how do you remain so calm?

It's not easy to stay calm, and even the very best players in the world struggle to keep all of their emotions in check from time to time. Tiredness will often play a major part. When you are short of breath, it affects your vision and you can't see the goal as well as you would when you are fresher at the start of the match. There are lots of factors. Maybe today I'll score a goal, but tomorrow I'll miss an easy chance. It happens. That's football. I wouldn't be human if I took all of my chances and that wouldn't be football. You can mess up sometimes and you can score sometimes, but the most important thing is that you react well after making a mistake and don't allow it to affect your confidence levels.

Are you the type of player that thrives under pressure during a big match?

I have to admit that I do feel pressure sometimes, but I like to feel that before a match because it allows me to enter the spirit of the game and adapt to the rhythm of the match quickly. But when you are out there on the pitch, whether you are playing against a big team like Manchester United in the League Cup final [in which Manolo scored twice at Wembley in February] or playing a side from the Championship, it's exactly the same because everything will disappear once the referee blows for kick-off. You just think about playing the game and you stop thinking about the pressure.

How do you adapt your game against different types of central defenders?

Here at Southampton we've got several performance analysts who all study our opponents and then show players some footage on an iPad. Before every match I like to watch videos of the goalkeeper, to see how he often moves for free-kicks and reacts to certain types of shot. I will also look at the defenders, to see if one of them is faster and one is slower. The objective is to try to find their weakest point and exploit that out on the pitch.

The Premier League is very physical, so did you do any additional work to get stronger before joining Saints?

No. When I first came here, I joined in with the usual training sessions and that's it. I have never been, and will never be, a big, bulky striker. The most important thing for me is that I am sharp in the final third of the pitch and very fast over short distances, so that I can pounce on any chances. I felt I already had that in Serie A, so didn't require extra sessions to get up to speed or anything like that.

THE DETAILS

The Italian talisman has got an eye for goal that runs in the family

Born
November 26, 1991

Birthplace
Calcinate, Lombardy

Clubs
Atalanta, Cittadella, Juventus, Bologna (loan), Sampdoria, Napoli, Southampton

Serie A goals
38 in 158 matches

International bow
England 2-1 Italy in August 2012

Italy record
Two goals in 11 Azzurri outings

Transfer fee
Southampton paid £14 million to sign him from Napoli

Admirers
West Ham, Spurs and Stoke were all linked with him in 2016. He returned to Sampdoria in 2019

Interview Paolo Bandini

masterclass

ALVARO MORATA

The Spanish goal-getter on his speed of thought, scoring with both feet and playing as a lone striker

A lot of elite strikers are blessed with pace – how are you still able to score so many goals without electric speed?

In the Premier League, you have much less time to think – one or two seconds is the difference between scoring a goal and not scoring, or making a good pass which results in a goal. To make up for that difference, you have to make your decisions as quickly as possible, because speed – whether it's in your head or feet – is key to being a successful striker. You must also be really intelligent with your movement and the runs you make. That can overcome a lot of things. A fast brain can be just as dangerous as a fast body.

So, is the Premier League much more about intuition than other countries?

To an extent. Part of your job is to think about what's going to happen next and try to anticipate other people's moves, because you know that anything could happen at any given moment. However, there is certainly less time to process all the information in front of you, so there are times when you play on instinct and your feel for a certain situation, based on the previous experiences in your career.

You have been likened to former Real Madrid frontman Fernando Morientes. What do you think about the comparison with your compatriot and how would you describe your style?

A lot of people have said that to me and I feel an awful lot of pride to be compared to such a fantastic centre-forward. As for me, I'd say that I am powerful, good when I've got my back to goal and a good finisher. The latter of those qualities is the most important. That's what being a striker is about: scoring with the fewest number of touches.

You're a very good finisher with both feet – how big an advantage is that?

It's huge. Logically, you have double the chance of scoring. It's the same with your head, which I've now spent many years working on in training. It's always been a part of the game which I've enjoyed, and if you really enjoy doing something, it no longer feels like work when you try to get better at it. If there's a secret to continuous improvement, then that's it.

There aren't many natural goalscorers left in the modern game – why do you think they've vanished over the years?

In the past you would have some much bigger strikers or forwards, whose only job was to score. But now teams need forwards to move around more, to look for the spaces between defenders and continually play with their back to goal. A centre-forward today has got to be a complete player, as football has evolved to one-striker formations which changes the way a team plays. A modern striker is so much more than just a goalscorer – they need to be able to set goals up and defend from the front as well.

Teams often choose to line up with one striker these days – what qualities do you need to be successful in this position?

You've got to be more intelligent than the defenders, above all else. I always try to stay on the move and lose my marker, which is the most important thing for a striker to do, other than actually scoring of course. If you are too static, it will be easy for two centre-backs to mark you and keep you out of the game. So, keep them guessing by moving into the areas which make them feel uncomfortable.

> **"You're like a VIP spectator playing in front of Iniesta, Silva, Isco, Mata... I only touch the ball to finish off a passing move"**

Spain play a short passing game, but your last three club sides – Juventus, Real Madrid and Chelsea – are usually more expansive. How does that alter the way you play for club and country?

It's just something you have to get used to. To a certain extent you have to keep switching your mentality, because the two styles are completely different. At Chelsea, and even with Real Madrid last season, the game is slightly crazier due to the importance of counter-attacking, but you have to be adaptable. For Spain, sometimes you find that the only time you touch the ball is to finish off a very long passing move. It's almost as if you are a VIP spectator when playing ahead of Isco, David Silva, Andres Iniesta and Juan Mata. They can all keep the ball so well that you end up nicking the ball off them and stopping their own game! It's such a brilliant team to play in, though.

As a striker, is it good to have a selfish streak when you're bearing down on goal? Do you need a specific type of personality to be a great goalscorer?

Sometimes you've got to be selfish, but sometimes not. I believe it's important that centre-forwards have anxiety about scoring goals for themselves, because that's their primary job out on the pitch. But you cannot be egotistical with your team-mates – you can only be one with the demands you place on yourself, in terms of the number of goals you try to score. At the end of the day, there's no specific type of person you've got to be to become a top goalscorer. Ultimately, you need to have the mentality to find the back of the net. I'm the sort of guy who always wants more. More goals. To train more. To improve more. I want to evolve as a footballer – it's that simple.

THE DETAILS

Right foot, left foot, header: the Spaniard can score all types of goals

Age
26

Shirt number
9

Premier League apps
47

Goals
16

Headers
7

Right foot
6

Left foot
3

Assists
6

Goals per game
0.34

Shooting accuracy
44%

*Up to January 14, 2019

Interview Andrew Murray

ALEX IWOBI

The Arsenal starlet explains how to add style and swagger to your game

How did you handle the pressure of making your debut last season?

Honestly, I wasn't nervous at all. There were a few other youngsters who were also making their debuts and wanted to impress, which probably took the pressure off me a little bit. The game [at Sheffield Wednesday in the League Cup] was on TV, so I was excited to get out there and show what I could do. I told myself to do the simple things well and I knew if I did that, then the rest of my game would come together. It was all a dream come true for me.

> "Confidence is key. When you have self-belief, you trust your ability and can take ownership of the game"

What advice did Arsene Wenger give you before the game at Hillsborough?

He just kept it really simple and didn't overcomplicate his message. He told everyone to enjoy themselves because that's the reason why we had started playing football in the first place. I think that helped to put myself and the rest of the boys at ease. Unfortunately we didn't get the result we wanted on the night, but it was a great learning curve.

How would you describe your style?

It's always hard talking about your own game, but I'd say I'm creative and I can score goals. My weakness is definitely heading. I can't head the ball at all, and always get stick for it at training. I also have a few tricks in my locker and I like making chances and setting up goals for my team-mates. I've played a lot of football this season and I want to start scoring a few more goals now that I've got some experience under my belt.

Do you need to have a certain type of personality to become a top player?

I think that confidence is massive. It's so important for every player. I don't think you can do really well in football without confidence. When you have more self-belief, you start to take risks and do things that you know you are capable of. You trust your ability more and you take more ownership of the game. Mental strength is also very important - every single player makes mistakes but you have to back yourself to get on the ball and make something happen the next time that you get it.

What advice would you tell a player who wants to become a professional?

The advice I've always been given is to just express myself and play the game with a smile on my face. You also have to listen to your coaches - they have years and years of experience and their knowledge will improve you as a player. It's important to believe in your ability as well - having that inner self-belief is something that you need when you are going through a bad run of form.

Lots of players sign professional contracts but don't fulfil their potential - why do you think you made it and others didn't?

When you're in the 16-18 age bracket it's more of a man's game, rather than just playing for fun. You have to mature quickly and have the right mental attitude in terms of actively improving your game every day. There is always someone else waiting to take your place - you have to make sure that you want it more than anybody else.

Arsenal's youth academy is full of different nationalities - has that cultural experience benefited you?

Definitely. You understand a lot more about how different teams play from different countries. Some players are more physical or technical, while other nationalities place more emphasis on tactics, so you gain an understanding of that through speaking to all of the players from various backgrounds in the dressing room. On a human level it's a good experience as well, as you get to find out how other people have grown up living in different countries. Jeff Reine-Adelaide was born in France and he's a good friend of mine. Initially, he couldn't speak much English and it was quite difficult to understand him, but he's really improved over time and I have started to speak a bit of French as well. I have learned a lot from him.

Are you the type of player who likes to use the gym to work on different areas of fitness during training?

I will probably train in the gym twice a week. When our games are coming thick and fast, we don't do anything too intense in the gym. When we do go in, it's predominantly to maintain the strength in our legs, because that is the part of the body we mainly use in football. I work on my hamstrings and quads. My hamstrings can get very stiff sometimes, so I'll often do some Romanian deadlifts to work on them. I really hate that exercise! I'm not a huge fan of the Bulgarian squats either, but I just grit my teeth and get on with them. A couple of days after the session you feel much stronger, and then you know that all of the hard work you've been doing in the gym has been worthwhile.

THE DETAILS

The young Gunner talks tricks, tunes & Will Smith

Favourite music
Wretch 32 – he is good lyrically.

Last album bought
Views by Drake.

Pre-match tune
All The Way Up by Fat Joe fires me up.

Favourite actor
Will Smith – I want to be just like him!

Pre-match meal
Carbs, carbs, carbs! Lots of rice or pasta.

Gym session or cardio session?
Gym. I hate cardio – we do hard sessions.

Favourite tricks
Flip-flap. I've pulled it off in training on a few occasions.

Five years from now you'll be...
Still at Arsenal and scoring plenty of goals, hopefully.

Interview Chris Flanagan

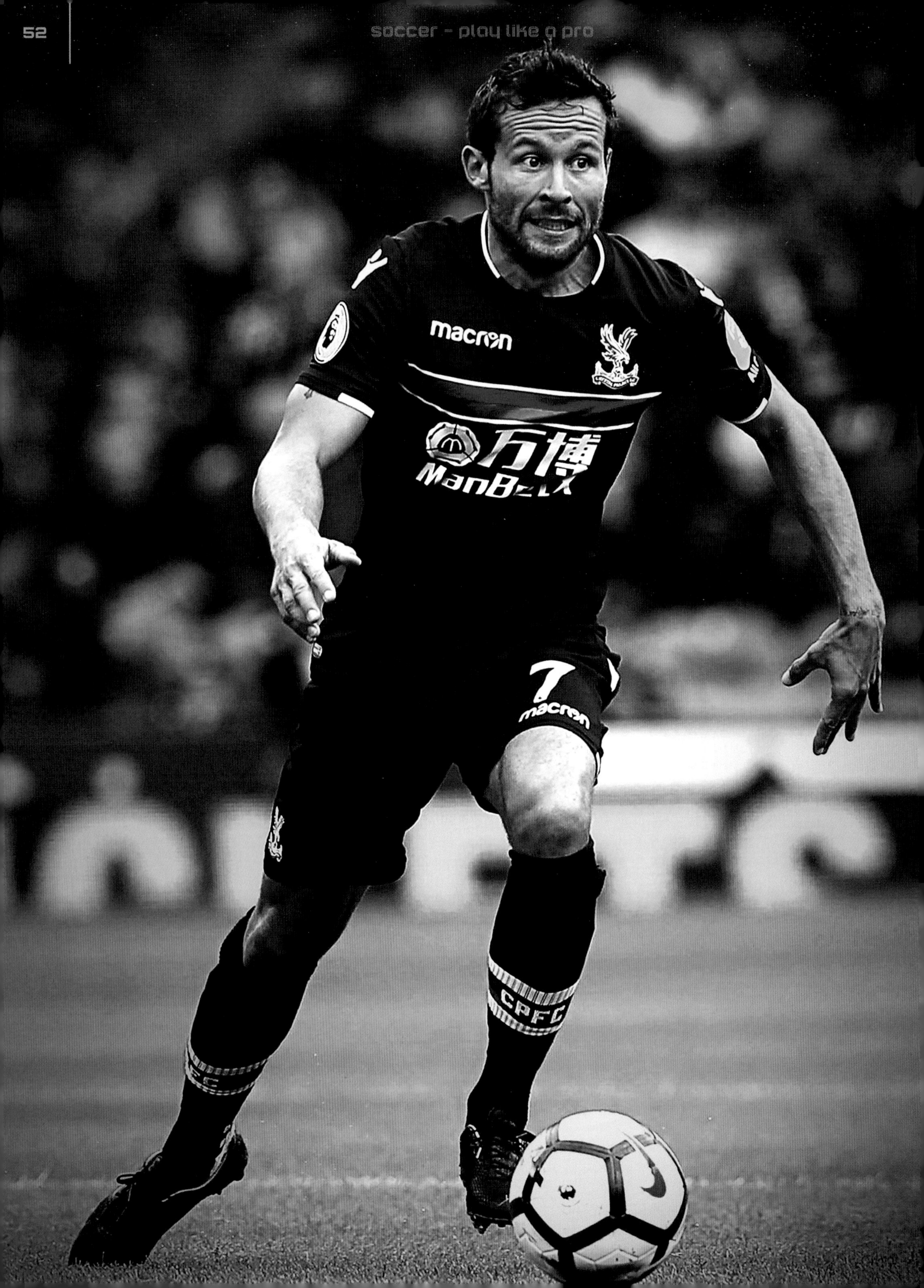
macron
万博
ManBetX
7
macron
CPFC

masterclass

YOHAN CABAYE

The classy playmaker on passing, the French production line and his admiration for Stevie G

Hi Yohan. Which midfielders did you admire when you were growing up?

I used to love watching Patrick Vieira and Claude Makelele play for France, as they were amazing together in midfield and controlled everything. I can remember the 2006 World Cup in Germany – they were fantastic in helping France reach the final. It's very rare that a country is able to produce two great midfielders in the same generation, but France did it – they complemented each other so well.

France have got a wealth of midfield talent at the moment – how do they keep finding so many top midfielders?

It's very hard to say. We have fantastic strikers and wingers as well. In general, the French academy system is of such an extremely high standard. It's really difficult being a young player at a club in France, but in a good way. There are so many talented players, meaning the competition is difficult. But that forces you to raise your game, otherwise you won't break through to the first team.

Passing has always been your biggest strength. Were you a naturally gifted passer or was it perfected over time?

For me, the most important part of the game is passing the ball – it's all about taking one touch and then making the right pass with the right weight. A killer pass, breaking the defensive lines, can send a team-mate through on goal and help your side to win the game. This is a part of my game that I've continually tried to develop over the years and I'm proud of the passer that I've become.

Who are the best passers that you've played against in the Premier League?

In my opinion, the best passer that I've played against and watched was Steven Gerrard, as I loved seeing him strike the ball. I could say many other players too, for example Xabi Alonso at Liverpool or Paul Scholes at Manchester United, but Gerrard is my favourite. His range of passing was fantastic – he could look up and pick out a team-mate from around 60 or 70 yards, and straight to their feet.

How do you control a game without being blessed with blistering pace?

All three of the players I just mentioned weren't particularly quick, but they were able to make up for it with the speed of their brain. Firstly, it's all about being in the right position when you receive the ball from your team-mate, preferably in space, and then having the ability to play a forward pass or a quick ball which will affect the opposition. You need to start by honing your passing range every day. Once you possess the technique to play a variety of quality passes consistently, and the intelligence to occupy the right areas, then you can start to run a game.

> "The best passer I've played against was Gerrard. He could look up and pick someone out from 60-70 yards – straight to feet"

You've scored some great free-kicks during your career. Can you tell us the secret to curling in a killer dead ball?

It's another part of my game, which I've tried to develop a lot since I was young. If you want to become a great free-kick taker, you have to practice every single day. That's what I do. I find setting myself individual challenges helps me to improve. I might have 10 balls and say to myself that I want to hit the top left corner with five of them. It keeps the brain thinking and working constantly. Free-kicks are really important because they can win a game in a second. If you're involved in a tight match and it's tough to score a goal in open play, a quality free-kick can be the difference sometimes. That's why it's so important to work on all your individual skills – they can give you an extra edge.

You have been deployed in defensive and offensive midfield roles – what is the difference between the positions?

When I play deeper I can touch the ball more often, but I also have to focus on the overall balance of the team. I can't get forward and join in with an attack if there are too many men committed up the pitch. I always have to look around me before making a decision – you have to use your brain in this role. When I'm playing as an attacking midfielder I can take more risks and make more runs into the penalty box, trying to score goals. In this position there is more responsibility on me to affect things in the final third, which means attempting through-balls and crosses, and having shots at goal.

Is good chemistry throughout a team essential to playing passing football?

I think it's important to be open with the other players and socialise with them, so that you can build up friendships. I think you need to speak not only to the senior players at a club, but those in the youth team as well. If and when they progress to the first team, there will already be an established connection in place, so you will communicate better on the pitch and speak the same football language. And if you know someone well, you'll want to fight for them on the pitch, too. You will also know how to speak to them during a game, to get the best out of them in certain situations.

Interview Alec Fenn

THE DETAILS

The French pass master averages one goal or assist in every four Prem outings

Age
33

Shirt number
7

First club
Lille

Premier League apps
175

Goals
26

Assists
15

Free-kicks
4

Total passes
7,100

Passes per match
40.57

Up to July 1, 2018

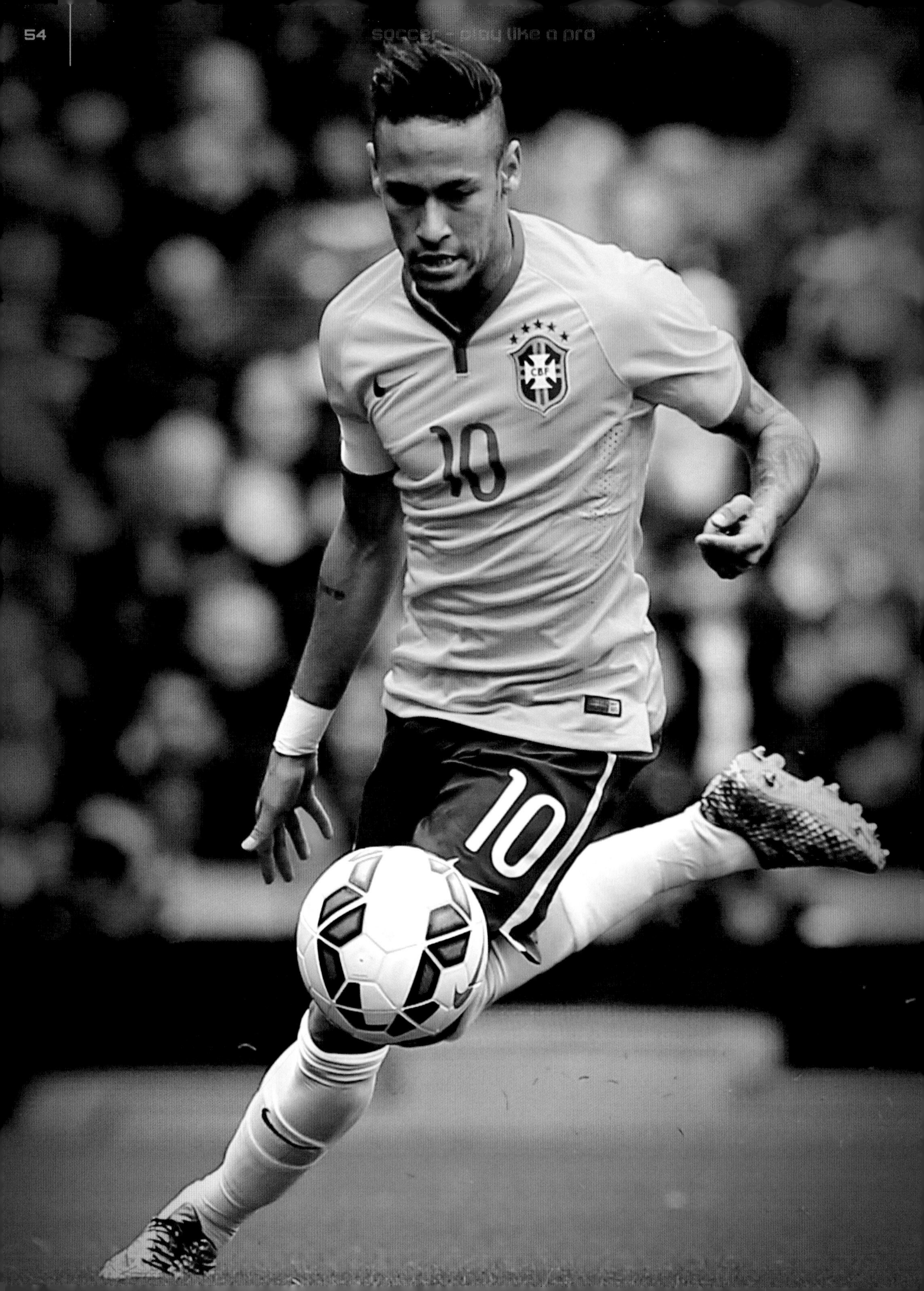
CBF
10
10

NEYMAR JR

The PSG and Brazil trickster on how street football influenced his game

How did street football shape the player you are today?
It definitely helped me to develop a fast game as well as that Brazilian smartness. I remember, as a child, I would wake up every morning and just want to play football, even though I knew I had to go to school. As soon as I arrived home I'd grab my football and go straight out, then play with my friends until late at night. Nothing else seemed to matter at that young age.

Did your coaches encourage you to play football on the streets?
No - quite the opposite. My coaches were scared I'd get injured and miss training or a game. That didn't stop me!

> "Futsal helped to develop my speed of thought. When Barcelona play, there's not much space so you need to react quickly"

Which coach has had the biggest influence on your career?
I've been lucky to play under so many great coaches who helped to improve my game in different ways, but the one I have the most affection for is [former Santos, Fluminense and Brazil player] Lima. He was my coach when I was a teenager. I had a real bond with him.

What do you remember of your professional debut for Santos at 17? How did you feel, walking out to a crowd chanting your name?
I didn't really know what to do! I didn't know whether to smile, applaud the crowd, wave my hands in the air or just stay serious. It feels quite complicated when you're that young, but I ended up playing that first game at the Pacaembu [Stadium] and the rest is history.

You're a very skilful player. How did you become the player you are today?
Futsal had a massive influence on me when I was growing up. It's a very demanding game and it really helped to develop my technique, my speed of thought and my ability to perform moves in tight spaces. I think futsal is a fundamental part of a footballer's life.

Why's that?
You're forced to think fast and move faster - if you lose a second, the ball will be gone. It's a more dynamic game, and it's come in handy at Barcelona. When we play, there's not much space so you need to react quickly. There's no doubt futsal has helped me a lot in my career. It's one of the biggest passions in my life. I used to love playing it, but unfortunately I had to stop at 13 or 14 in order to grow up as a footballer.

What are your fondest memories of that time in your life?
I can remember being just seven years old when I won my first individual award, which was a pretty special feeling as a child. I was making my debut for Portuguesa [Santista], another club from Santos city, and we finished third in a futsal tournament. I scored 23 goals.

Was it difficult to make the move from futsal to football?
Not really. I started playing football from the age of 11, before combining the two until I was 14. There then came a point where I couldn't play both anymore and had to choose. Of course, I chose football. It's funny: I can still remember my father watching my futsal games and making comments about how I played, even when I was very young. He was always there, following everything I did.

Who is your futsal idol?
It has to be [Brazilian futsal legend] Falcao. He's one of the athletes who inspires me the most. We have a very close relationship – he's one of those people who walk into your life and you want to keep them. However, besides being my friend, he's also an outstanding player – the best of all time. He was meant to be here [at Neymar Jr's five-a-side tournament in Praia Grande, Brazil] but unfortunately it wasn't possible. If he was here, he would have played for my team!

What advice would you give to a young street footballer who wants to become a professional footballer?
It's very hard to give advice to young players. You see a lot of youngsters who have potential, but for various reasons they don't reach their goals. It's quite sad when that happens, but from my experience, if you've got the same dream I had as a child then there are certain things you need to do. You have to stay focused at all times and ignore any distractions. Also, ensure you always remain attached to your family. You must trust them. It is important to keep all of your closest friends around you as well - that's another big thing. And on the pitch, always give everything and train hard. Do all of those things, and you'll give yourself a chance.

Neymar Jr was talking at the World Final of his global five-a-side event.

Interview Marcus Alves

masterclass

JUAN MATA

The playmaker reveals how to give big defenders the slip

Hola, Juan. How does a small player such as yourself survive in a division as physical as the Premier League?

It's a good question! In England there are many big and strong players, which means that I have to think a bit more, because of the big difference in size between myself and a lot of players. If you're not tall or strong you have to move earlier and try to find the spaces before your rival. The mental side of the game is really important for the smaller players – if you try to stand toe-to-toe with a bigger man, it's very difficult to come out on top.

> "I have to think more, playing in England: if you aren't tall or strong, you must move earlier and try to find spaces"

Do you adapt your game against fast or strong defenders?

It depends on whether you have the ball or the defender has the ball. If he has possession, I make sure I'm smart tactically and pick up good positions to stop him from running into space or making a key pass. If I have the ball, I make sure my first touch is good – that's really important. I also like to play one-twos with my team-mates, trying to draw him out of position. It's all about tricking him, and you have to think really quickly.

You're very good at finding little pockets of space in a match - is that something you work on?

When I'm looking to find some space in which to receive the ball, some of that is instinctive. I have a natural feel now for where the ball is going to go, because I have played the game for so many years. However, this is still something that you can practise in training. I know it sounds like really obvious advice, but you need to think: where can I position my body to receive the ball best? Where is there likely to be more space? It's important to have a good sense of orientation, as this will enable you to make the right decisions in different areas of the pitch and be decisive when the time comes.

What's the secret to keeping possession in tight spaces?

You need to look around – 360 degrees – all the time before you receive the ball. You need to know where you are, where your team-mates are and where the opposition players are. When you watch Spanish players, you'll see they always do this. Xavi is probably the very best in the world at it. He is not that quick physically, but he's extremely quick in his mind and that's one of the key qualities that great players possess.

Do you work on strength in the gym?

I use the gym three times per week, but it always depends on how many games we have. If we have two or three games in quick succession, we can't do too much, as we need to focus on recovery. We do sessions that work both the legs and the upper body. Even though I'm physically tiny I still make sure I do my physical work as well, so that I avoid injuries and have a good base level of strength with which to shield the ball.

Are there any exercises you think are important for playmakers?

There are many areas of fitness that you need to work on. I do a lot of core and co-ordination work – I think it's good to work on the link between the brain and your legs and feet. I also focus on reaction work for the feet and jumping exercises to improve power. I believe in fitness that is specific for the pitch. I always want to do things that I am going to be repeating during a match. You must train physically, but orientated towards the game.

What do you do to help your body recover after training or a match?

When I lived in Spain I enjoyed an afternoon siesta, but it's something I've stopped doing since I moved to England because the culture is very different. I recover by doing lots of stretching and pool work, transferring between hot and cold water. I also eat lots of quality food to make sure I recover from training and games as quickly as possible. You can't get away with eating and drinking whatever you want – if you want a long career at the top level, you have to be disciplined.

What types of food do you eat in order to fuel your performance?

I eat breakfast at the training ground and normally I'll have some toast and a banana so that I have plenty of carbohydrates in my system before training. I also like a glass of orange juice, and a coffee to wake me up. We have a great chef, Mike, who makes fish dishes at lunchtime. I often eat salmon and pasta, particularly before matches. It's a meal that has always made me feel really energetic before I play. Drinking lots of water is also key as it helps to keep me hydrated. At home, I like to cook something myself for dinner. A dish I eat a lot is fabada, which is a rich Spanish bean stew. It's probably my biggest meal of the day and keeps me full before bed.

Juan Mata is the first global ambassador for streetfootballworld, a non-profit organisation which works with over 100 companies across 67 countries to help 1.2 million young people through football

THE DETAILS

A Mata of fact: here are 10 things you didn't know about him

Dream coffee date
Eric Cantona

Studying
Sports science and marketing degrees

Favourite film
Midnight in Paris

Childhood idol
Diego Maradona

Best friend
Granada's David Lomban

Foible
Can't fall asleep if he doesn't set an alarm

Superstition
He always puts on his left boot first

Dream signing for Manchester United
Andres Iniesta

Second sport
Table tennis

If he wasn't a footballer...
He'd work in advertising

Interview Alec Fenn

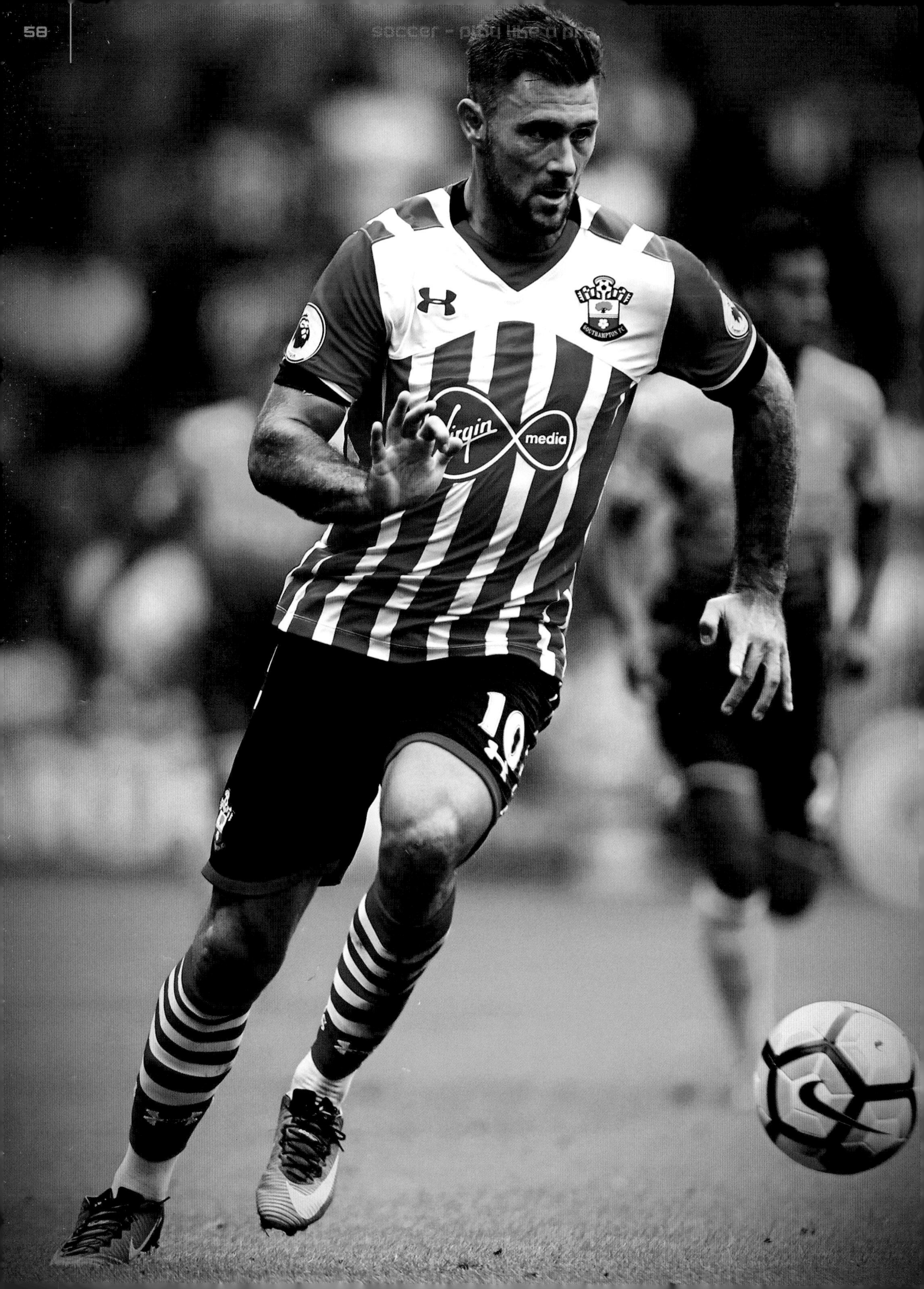
SOUTHAMPTON FC
Virgin media

CHARLIE AUSTIN

The Southampton striker talks tricking defenders and finishing with aplomb

Hi Charlie. What advice can you give us to help improve our finishing?

Hi. It's all about composure. When you're in front of goal, don't panic. I think a lot of people get into that position and then freeze and take too long. If you're one-on-one with the keeper, it's important that you don't change your mind. If you feel like you're going to go round him, go round him. If you feel like you're going to take an early shot, then go and do it. If you want to chip him, do that. All of my finishing is about committing to it – relax, pick your spot and commit.

> "You can trick a defender by pretending to switch off. You're playing a game of cat and mouse"

What's your favourite way to score?

They all count, so for me it's probably a nice first-time finish in the box. It's easy to say it's beating three men and putting the ball in the top corner from 30 yards, but it doesn't really happen. But a nice cross in and a header, or a good first touch and a controlled finish, is what I do most often.

How important is movement when you're trying to lose a defender?

Movement is massive and I think it's something many players neglect. You have to make a movement towards or away from a defender to create space for yourself. You need to be on the move at all times. You can trick a defender by pretending to switch off, and as much as a defender thinks you're switching off, you're not. You can walk around looking uninterested and then bang – you're away. You're playing a game of cat and mouse with the defender, and that's how I work.

Do you have to be selfish to succeed as a striker?

Of course. Every time I go on the pitch, I think I am going to score. If you don't think like that then you doubt yourself. Every time I play, I think I'm going to score a goal or that a chance is going to come my way. If that chance doesn't come off, then I think another one will come along soon. If I'm on the bench and I feel like I'm going to come on, I always think of that one chance and make sure I'm ready for it. It might be a half-chance or a

quarter-chance but you have to be ready to put the ball away. OK, when you're one-on-one with the goalkeeper and your team-mate is right there, you slide him in – it's a team game – but for a striker it's all about goals. Strikers are judged on goals.

Have you got to be willing to take a bit of flak from your team-mates for shooting instead of passing?

Definitely. When you don't pass and you don't score, then it's possible that you've ignored the better option. But as a centre-forward, if you run through on goal, take your shot and score, then all your team-mates are happy and celebrating, so it's a catch-22 situation. But that is where the selfishness comes into it – you have to believe that you'll score when you get the chance.

Which strikers did you idolise as a child?

Ruud van Nistelrooy, Alan Shearer and the Brazilian Ronaldo. Van Nistelrooy scored goals for fun and yet I think he only scored about five from outside the box in his whole career. That just shows what a clinical finisher he was. I remember asking Rio [Ferdinand] about him at QPR. He said if people weren't crossing the ball in, Ruud would tell them he needed it in the box, because they had someone strong in there.

If you look at Alan Shearer, he was an old-fashioned No.9 and was just superb. He wore the armband for his country and was a player that I looked up to, as he was the top scorer almost every season. He scored 260 Premier League goals, and I don't think that number will ever be beaten.

Then you take Ronaldo: he played for Brazil, Milan, Inter, Real Madrid, Barcelona – you have to wonder how good he would have been if he didn't have the injuries. He was special and an expert when he was one-on-one with the keeper. Whether it was with a double step-over, a single step-over, the flip-flap – he had so much variety. For me, he was the ultimate finisher.

Who is the toughest centre-back you've ever come up against?

Phil Jagielka. When I played against him for QPR at home to Everton he was very good. I thought, 'Wow, I really need to be on my game here' and I didn't play well on the day. You go away thinking that the next time you face him, you'll have a right go. I don't think he'll mind me saying he's not blessed with pace, but I have spoken about strikers' movements and he read the game really well. As a forward, my movement had to be at the top of my game to get any chances against him.

Interview Ben Welch

THE DETAILS

Eight facts on the brickie who became a top-flight marksman

Age
29

Height
6ft 2in

First Football League goal
For Swindon at Carlisle in 2009

Favourite goal
An extra-time tap-in for QPR to beat Wigan in the 2014 Championship play-off semi-final

Pre-match playlist
"Oasis, Drake and Bastille are three of my favourites"

Favourite tune
"I like *Champagne Supernova* by Oasis – hearing it means it's time to get to work"

Pre-match meal
"Pasta, chicken and a bit of pesto. It's boring, really"

Treat food
Katsu curry

NATHAN REDMOND

The Southampton flyer on adapting to the No.10 role and leaving defenders for dead

You've played off the striker this season – how have you found it?
It's been a good learning curve for me. I've mainly played as a winger in my career, but the manager has asked me to play in a more central role this season and it's something I have enjoyed. If I'm able to play in any position across the front four, it means that I give him more options.

What attributes must you have in order to become an effective No.10?
You need to be the link man between the midfield and attack. It's important to stay close to the striker as well and play around him. Your responsibility is to create assists and score goals. You need to always be on the lookout for space to get on the ball, so that you can feed the striker and two wingers.

> "I loved watching Ronaldinho and Henry, but these days I try to take bits from Pedro and Willian and use them myself"

Is there also additional defensive responsibilities in this position?
Definitely. As soon as you don't have the ball you've got to work with your striker to press the centre-backs and unsettle them. And you also need to be aware of your position in relation to midfielders behind you – if there is too much space, the other team's playmaker could do some damage.

Is it more difficult to find space compared to when you're out wide?
You will always find space if you drift and have team-mates who know how to draw defenders out of their comfort zone. There is a lot more balls into feet and one- and two-touch play as a No.10 – and you have to move the ball around really quickly and make fast decisions.

Which position is physically harder – attacking midfielder or winger?
It can be a long afternoon when you're playing out wide, as most full-backs you come up against in the Premier League are attack-minded and you've got to be careful not to leave your wing exposed. Positioning is so important – if you have a good understanding of exactly where you need to be at certain points of play, then you don't have to run quite as far.

Do you think it's vital for attacking midfielders to contribute goals?
Yes, it's been a big target of mine this season. I know I need to score more and I've put myself under pressure to do so. When I've gone through spells where I haven't been scoring I've not worried, as I'm confident that if I keep occupying the right spaces then I will. The manager says he'll only be worried if I'm not getting into the right areas.

How important is it to vary the way that you attack opposition defenders?
It's huge for wide players. When I play on the wing I like to drift inside off the touchline, pick the ball up in between the lines and keep opponents guessing. Sometimes I will dart back outside or play a quick one-two, which gives my team-mates different options to find me and stops me being predictable.

Defenders hate coming up against pace - is it the same for wingers?
It can be, yes. If a defender is not the quickest, sometimes all you need is a burst of acceleration to get away from him. If he's fast, it can develop into a game of cat and mouse as you know that physically he'll be capable of keeping up with you. In the modern game, though, you need more than just speed if you are going to be a top winger.

Do you study any other attacking players to improve your skill set?
Yeah. When I was younger I loved to watch Thierry Henry, Ronaldinho and the Brazilian Ronaldo, but I still watch and appreciate players that I come up against these days. People like Pedro, Willian and Manuel Lanzini, as well as [Lionel] Messi and Neymar, are brilliant at beating men in different ways, and I certainly look at each of them and try to take bits and bobs from their games.

How much of your training would you say is focused on your own game? Do you analyse opposition defenders?
I mainly focus on watching clips of the opposition's defensive unit. I will look for any trends in the way they operate and learn if there are any weaknesses that I can exploit. I also like to watch individual clips of both full-backs and the central defenders, so I can work out what their positioning is like and the way they play out from the back. I'm never too worried about watching footage of them going forward – I'm concerned with how I can hurt them.

Who is the toughest defender that you've faced in your career so far?
When I was only 17 or 18, Birmingham played Chelsea twice in the FA Cup and I found Branislav Ivanovic very difficult to play against, as he was so physically dominating and very big for a full-back. I was still a boy at that time. Then there was Bacary Sagna who used to bomb up and down for 90 minutes. The two seasons I was in the Championship, taking on defenders who are far more aggressive than those in the Premier League, really helped me adapt to playing against the different types of full-backs, and then develop some different ways of beating them.

Interview Alec Fenn

THE DETAILS

The Saints man's key numbers & milestones

Age
24

Birthplace
Birmingham

Height
5ft 8in

Squad number
22

Positions
Winger (left/right), attacking midfield

Professional debut
Birmingham 3-2 Rochdale (League Cup - 2010-11)

First goal
Birmingham 3-0 Nacional (Europa League - 2011-12)

Transfer fee
Saints signed him from Norwich for £10 million in 2016

England U21 appearances
38

England caps
1

Honours
England U21 Player of the Year - 2016

train like a pro

BRING BACK
THE BLEEP TEST,
gaffer!

An old-school boot camp in the Lake District is whipping players into shape ready for the new season – FFT joins Sheffield Wednesday's U23 squad for the toughest 24 hours of their lives

Words Alec Fenn **Photography** Tommy Martin, Chris West

t's a Friday afternoon and a teenager is hanging off the back of a large paddleboard, thrashing his legs in the water in an attempt to swim out to sea. Seven of his mates, armed with paddles, banter and a smattering of sleeve tattoos, sway from side to side, rowing in a disorderly fashion.

But these aren't British holidaymakers getting prepared for a booze cruise in Magaluf. Sheffield Wednesday's under-23 players are only drunk on fatigue as they face the final task on a punishing boot camp in the Lake District. They have been pushed to breaking point.

Their toil began the previous evening on a lawn outside of Graythwaite Hall – a Georgian building set in 5,000 acres of privately owned countryside. This is the home of Cassius Camps, an old-school pre-season training base where they have been sent to push their minds and bodies to the limit before the start of the new season. *FFT* has joined them for the ride.

The surroundings may be idyllic, but for the next 24 hours the players will live a much more primitive existence. The entire squad will sleep together in the same room, while their no-frills meals will only serve as fuel for the rigours of what is to come. Access to Wi-Fi is forbidden and free time used to reflect on their efforts.

The camp was born five years ago, when its founder Phil Ercolano brought four youngsters to the Lakes to take part in an experimental programme aimed at accelerating their development. They each set a target of making one first-team outing by the end of the campaign. Twelve months on, Calum Chambers, Morgan Fox, Josh Brownhill and Frankie Sutherland had got 70 between them.

A host of Football League outfits and individual players have since headed north to find out its secrets. Hung up on an office wall is a framed shirt from Southampton's Sam McQueen, plus a message written in black ink: 'Thanks for changing my life.' A day earlier, Sam completed a three-day camp for the second consecutive year. Last season, Carlisle – who will return in a few weeks – and AFC Fylde had two of the three longest unbeaten runs in England after visiting here. Barnsley and Walsall are also pencilled in for trips in the near future.

Ten outdoor challenges are available to clubs and players. Each one is built upon 12 improvement pillars: physical performance, mental strength, team relationships, leadership, communication, self-belief, self-awareness, motivation, career-life balance, self-discipline, values and personal brand. Every player is asked to give themselves a score out of five for each one both before and after.

These pillars were devised by Ercolano based upon his experiences in developing talent and his observations of world-class performers. He was signed up by Burnley when he was 16, only for a knee injury to rob him of a prosperous career in the game. Instead, he reinvented himself in the commercial world and spent a decade as the leader of several sports and media organisations in London. *FFT* has also learnt that he spent a period working as a model, during which he turned down a role in legendary pop band S Club 7.

"If you look at an elite performer such as Cristiano Ronaldo or the Leicester City team who won the Premier League, they both possess all of those qualities," says Ercolano. "A lot of these players won't have a career in football, but I firmly believe that if you can score highly in those 12 areas you will be a successful person, whether that is on the pitch, boardroom or in your personal life."

Wednesday's youngsters will undergo the 'Pushing the Limits Test' and 'The Cassius Challenge', but none of them have been told what each entails. Their stay starts with an evening team-building exercise. Ercolano, an athletic figure with dark hair, instructs two teams of six players try to form a rectangle formation with a long piece of rope while blindfolded. The aim is to improve their communication skills.

Technology has proven to be a big stumbling block in the Owls' development of

Clockwise from bottom
The Owls are blindfolded;
woken up at an ungodly
hour; wheeled out for lots of
heavy-lifting; and made to
communicate with one
another at the punishing
Lake District boot camp

"SOME OF YOU SAID THAT YOUR COMMUNICATION SKILLS WERE FIVE OUT OF FIVE – WELL THAT'S COMPLETE BOLLOCKS! IF YOU CARRY ON LIKE THIS, YOU'LL END UP PLAYING IN NON-LEAGUE"

round for a debrief. "Some of you said your communication skills were five out of five – that is complete bollocks! If you continue like this, you will end up playing in non-league or not at all."

The players retire to a dining room overlooked by hunted stag heads. There are three tables; two for the players and one for staff. Dinner is meat skewers, served with potatoes and vegetables. An old friend of the camp has been invited in to join them and deliver a talk to emphasise the difficult realities of life in football and the importance of showing resilience when life deals you a bad hand.

Rochdale midfielder Joe Thompson has been in remission for just two weeks after recovering from cancer for the second time in three years, but hobbles to the front of the room to tell his story. He was first diagnosed with the illness in 2013 while at Tranmere and was then released by the club as he made his recovery. Remarkably, he fought back to win a contract with Carlisle after impressing gaffer Keith Curle with his efforts at Cassius Camps, only to be diagnosed with the illness for a second time.

"Life and football can be a dark place," he tells *FFT* after receiving a rousing reception from Wednesday's youngsters. "If I didn't have the mental strength and self-belief, there is no way that I could have had a career or recovered from cancer. I was in isolation for 18 days receiving chemotherapy, but made it home much sooner than the doctors had first thought. It'll take time but I'm going to play again – my aim is to play next season."

It's 6:30am the following morning and Wednesday's youngsters are woken abruptly by *FFT*'s photographer, who charges into their living quarters and begins snapping their weary faces. "That was the worst night's kip of my life," says an unhappy camper. "My hamstrings have seen better days," moans another.

Over breakfast, *FFT* wonders which players will have what it takes to conquer the challenge ahead. Jordan Thorniley is a 20-year-old centre-back built like an outhouse, but he's slept for just two hours on a kitchen table such was his discomfort in the blow-up bed. I'm interested to find out just how far I can push myself," he says. "I hope this will help my self-awareness and reveal where I need to improve."

Deon Moore is slumped in his chair with his eyes shut and his hands down his pants. The 18-year-old is currently on trial with Wednesday after leaving Peterborough United and knows a good performance at the camp could earn him a deal. "I've heard about this place from lads at other clubs – they all said it was the hardest thing they have ever done," he says. "I want to get a bit of fitness in the bank and it will be a good way to get to know the lads."

Alex Hunt may well be the most streetwise. The 17-year-old has got a slender frame that doesn't really look built for boot camps, but this is going to be his second visit here inside 12 months. "I'm a lot better at handling bad results and situations," he explains. "I have warned the other lads about what's to come, and tried to visualise last year in my

young players. The club's former under-18 boss Danny Cadamarteri, who joined Burnley this summer, banned his squad from using their smartphones at the training ground and brought them to the camp last year in a bid to improve team spirit. "Football dressing rooms have become anti-social environments – you don't see big personalities such as Roy Keane or Patrick Vieira any more," Cadamateri reveals to *FFT*. "One of the reasons we took them there was to test them socially away from the modern world."

Neil Thompson is also concerned his under-23 players are not as vocal as those from previous eras. "If you look at players on the bus on the way to a game, they've all got headphones in or are playing games on their phones," he says, as his squad struggle to navigate their task. "They're afraid to speak up to the whole group if there's a problem, but you can't take your smartphone out on the pitch. Years ago you had to speak to each other and that is where you developed communication skills. Hopefully this will improve them."

But Ercolano is unhappy with the early efforts from his newest recruits. It's the first time that two teams have failed the task and he issues a blunt warning as the players gather

head – you really need the support of your team-mates to help you get through it all."

The first challenge of the morning is a one-and-a-half-mile run with a twist. The players will set off at 15-second intervals, aiming to hunt down the man in front, to encourage healthy inter-squad competition which they will all need to secure their place this season. A handful of marshals are dotted around the course, but the players have all been told to memorise their route or risk becoming lost in the countryside. A recent visit from rugby league outfit St Helens saw some members of the squad spend four hours stranded after taking a wrong turn.

With a week of pre-season training already under their belts, the run will provide another marker of each player's fitness and an early insight into their mindset. "Some of you will be thinking, 'I'm a baller, I play for Sheffield Wednesday'," says Ercolano, with a look of disdain. "You'll get nowhere with that attitude. Will you accept a narrow win with a head start or will you empty the tank to catch the guy in front?"

FFT is excited to watch the race unfold and jumps in Ercolano's 4x4, which will act as the pacemaker at the front of the pack. Slowly but surely he drives through a roller coaster of country roads, with his car window wound down so he can bark out encouragement and ensure there is no slacking in the impressive pace being set by the academy's performance analyst, Mark Rudd. "Keep going! Dig in! Don't let your team-mate catch up!"

One by one, each player arrives at the finish line, soaked in sweat and grimacing as the reality of the camp's intensity begins to dawn. The early-morning run has merely served as a warm-up for the most brutal test of the day – a timed obstacle course so punishing that it reduced a rugby player to tears and has forced many others to vomit. Three players at a time must bear-crawl down individual lanes before completing 15 stations. The toughest requires them to flip and deadlift tyres, press massive logs above their heads, carry water canisters and push wheelbarrows full of sandbags down the course.

This has been designed by the camp's performance director, Adam Smith. He understands the demands of elite sport having previously worked with the New Zealand All Blacks and England's rugby union team. "This has been designed to break them mentally, emotionally and spiritually – we want to see how they deal with it," he explains.

Clockwise from top left Wednesday's under-23s endure an unforgiving uphill challenge; after a slightly less gruelling team-building exercise; a sweaty Warren Clarke digs deep to haul a log up yet another hill; the young players face their fears with the final test – paddling to the middle of Lake Windermere and then swimming to shore

"This will weed out the weakest members of the group."

One player who quickly finds himself in deep water is Jack Stobbs. The 20-year-old enjoyed a summer holiday shortly before the camp, after signing a new one-year deal in June, and appears to have paid the price. His face turns beetroot-red as his progress repeatedly grinds to a halt while hauling a sandbag, one-handed like a suitcase, down his lane. His struggle prompts a few team-mates to rally round and shout encouragement to get him over the line, which he eventually crosses well after his two

Smith. "The best players I've worked with are emotionally stable. Jonny Wilkinson and Dan Carter could deal with stressful situations incredibly well."

FFT feels sorry for Thorniley's team-mate, Sean Clare, who has to carry more than 14 stones' worth of centre-back up a hill. Facing an equally difficult mission is Hunt, whose skinny legs will surely buckle as he strives to make it to the top. As the task begins, the sound of rallying cries drown out the grunting and groaning as the squad pull together and realise they're stronger when working as a sum of their parts. Remarkably, both Clare and Hunt pull through and then act as cheerleaders to encourage their partner.

It's a timely display of togetherness ahead of their final challenge. The squad is split into two teams, and they must paddleboard to the middle of Lake Windermere before jumping into the water and swimming to shore. Once on dry land, their weary legs are tasked with carrying them to their base, through a series of hilly lanes that will push them to breaking point. The water provides what Ercolano calls 'lightbulb' moments, when the players conquer their fears and managers realise who they can count on when things gets tough.

Two years ago, Carlisle striker Jabo Ibehre stunned boss Curle by diving into the water and crawling his way to shore, despite being unable to swim. He later credited the camp for inspiring the best campaign of his career in front of goal, aged 32. The trialist Michael Cregan is faced with the same inner battle after revealing that he's never learned to swim. "I just don't work properly in water," laughs the Irishman. The camp's staff refuse to force him into a decision, but with manager Thompson watching and a contract on the line, he takes a deep breath and embarks the paddleboard out to the lake.

Twenty minutes later, a sea of bodies slowly approach land. Most are unsteady on their feet, but they muster the energy for the final mile-long run back to the hall. However, one player is missing. In the distance, FFT can just about see Cregan thrashing and splashing as he tries to gather pace. Eventually, long after his team-mates have returned, he emerges from the water. His efforts earn a pat on the back from Ercolano, who jumps in his car to follow the youngster up the hill to ensure that he continues running. This is injury-time and he is making sure he sees the game out.

The day finishes with a debrief and highlights reel showing the boys overcoming each task. The trip has been a learning curve for all. "I've realised size doesn't matter – mental strength is more important than physical strength," says Hunt. Thorniley's gained the self-awareness he craved. "It's the hardest thing I've done, but now I feel ready to go on loan and take the next step in my career." Thompson is proud of his players. "They have shown they can really dig in, which will help us in the final 20 minutes of matches." Ercolano has one final piece of advice. "Good luck, have a great season and go and "batter some teams".

rivals in a time of 20 minutes.

His performance is then put to shame by Moore and Thorniley, who power through the pain barrier to complete the course in 14 and 15 minutes respectively, putting the pair among the leading times ever recorded at Cassius Camps. Equally impressive is the effort of Hunt, who clocks 19 minutes despite his vastly inferior size, which wins the respect of camp staff and a nod of approval from his manager.

...

After a brief break, the squad embark on their second run of the day that is entirely uphill and must be completed while also carrying a log in both hands. Once at the top, the group poses for a picture before walking back to their base, with lunch marking the camp's halfway stage. It's at this point that excuses begin to emerge, as two players complain of minor knocks. FFT asks Ercolano if there is a difference between the mentality of Premier League players and those lower down the pyramid. "You get this on every camp, whatever their level," he says with a shake of the head. "But you normally get three who display the physical and mental strength to make it to the very top."

The squad will require great fortitude for their final two activities, the first of which is a military-type exercise requiring them to run up a steep hill while carrying one of their team-mates. Once they reach the summit, each pair returns to the bottom and then swap roles. The task is then completed by sprinting downhill one last time and bear-crawling back up this punishing patch of terrain. "We often see players lose their heads," says

the winter workout

Make the most of the wintry weather when it hits with seasonal exercises from elite performance coach Nick Grantham

PUDDLE HOPS

Stand side-on to a puddle. Jump across width-ways on your outside leg, landing on your other leg, and jump back to and fro. Bend your knees to enable you to spring. "In icy conditions these are known as skater hops," says Grantham. "They are great for single-leg stability and strength, which help with changes of direction."

PUDDLE JUMP

Find a large puddle – if it's icy be careful – and stand at one end, feet slightly apart. Take off with both feet, swinging your arms and bending your knees to drive yourself over the puddle before landing on both feet. "This is good to develop horizontal power, which helps with your initial 3-5 strides of acceleration in a match," adds Grantham.

SNOWBALL FIGHT

Let's face it: if it snows or you're going skiing, you're probably going to be doing this anyway. Make a bunch of snowballs and then let battle commence. Says Grantham: "This is great for working on agility, developing rapid reaction and movement as you try to avoid getting hit."

SANDBAG CARRIES

Putting up the flood barriers provides physical benefits, too. "Having to constantly stabilise your body as the sand – and the weight – moves around will give you a full workout," explains Grantham, who counts elite basketball players and the RFU among his clients.

Words Louis Massarella; **Illustration** Jason Pickersgill

CHOPPING LOGS

Stand with your feet shoulder-width apart and your back straight. Swing the axe above your head and let it rip! "Cutting wood for the fire is a great rotational exercise, working the upper and lower body as well as the core," says our conditioning coach.

LOG DEADLIFT

Holding a log across your shoulders, keep your back and neck straight, squat and stand up. Take care to stay balanced. "This exercise will work the whole body – even better if you are carrying the log over to the fire," explains Grantham, who has trained Olympic athletes.

SLED PULLS

Get your kids, somebody else's kids, or even just something heavy on the sled, tow them 20 metres, turn around and repeat. "This lower-body exercise can be done even if doesn't snow," says Grantham. "It is a good exercise to build up acceleration."

HEAVY GOING LUNGES

Find a boggy area of the ground. Step forward with one leg, bend and descend until your other knee nearly touches the ground, then proceed forward with the other leg and repeat. As Grantham says, "This will help improve your explosive power, helped by the ground's resistance."

CAR PUSHES

Cars aplenty get stuck in the mud or snow at this time of year – do your bit and help to push them out. "Keep a 45-degree body angle and drive hard with each stride, fully extending each leg. Like a sprinter flying out of the blocks, this is really good for your acceleration."

SNOW SHOVELLING

Load up the shovel, rotate one way and launch the snow in one direction, then repeat, rotating the other way. Soil works, too. "As anybody who's done a bit of digging knows, this is a full body workout, good for working the whole core," says Grantham, a former strength and conditioning coach at the English Institute of Sport.

Our expert says: "You can do all or some of these exercises in a circuit if you like. Otherwise, when using an external load, try lifting something that makes 10 repetitions challenging. For the other exercises, work for 40 seconds and rest for 20 between each set. Do as many sets as you can manage."

Nick Grantham is the author of *The Strength & Conditioning Bible: How to Train Like an Athlete* (Bloomsbury)

TRAIN LIKE A PRO

The ultimate workouts to get you looking and feeling like a pro

"Battle ropes are used by players as part of metabolic conditioning sessions, to increase caloric burn and maintain lean muscle"

CHARLTON ATHLETIC'S FIRST TEAM SPORT SCIENTIST JOSH HORNBY

HOW TO...
loosen up your limbs

Activate your muscles before a game by mastering this resistance band routine from Brentford's strength and conditioning coach, Tom Perryman

1 Leg lower

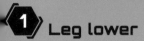

We've seen enough players crippled by chocolate hamstrings and don't want you to be next. "This exercise mimics the running and striking motions that you produce over and over in games," says Perryman. "One hip is flexed and the other is loose. You should also feel a nice abdominal contraction if you do it slowly."

**ALL EXERCISES
3 SETS
5-10 REPS**

2 Romanian deadlift

If you've got hips stiffer than a rusty car door, you won't be able to change direction. "This is an excellent hip-hinge movement and will loosen the posterior chain – the muscles on the rear of your lower body. It's great for improving balance and preparing you for single-leg moves in a match."

3 Glute band squat

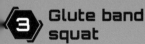

Prepare to leap off the ground and dominate the skies with this glute-burning routine. "Keep your legs wide and resist the pressure of the band, which tries to pull your knees back in. Go as deep as you possibly can while maintaining a good form. Avoid bending over too far and arching your back."

4 Single leg push-out

To ensure your whole lower body is switched on and ready for action, you can't neglect your calves. "Wrap the band around the top part of your foot and push against it. The resistance targets your calves and prepares them to be stable and strong when pushing against the grass."

5 Glute band walks

Don't run before you can walk with a resistance band wrapped around your ankles. You might pull a muscle, and we don't want that. "Side-to-side movements will activate your hips and abductors. Try moving around in a square to mimic your movements out on the pitch."

TRAIN LIKE A PRO

The ultimate workouts to get you looking and feeling like a pro

"Upper body power is crucial today. A wide arm pull-up will work on the trapezius and latissimus dorsi muscles"

JOHN HARTLEY, ASTON VILLA'S
IN JURY PREVENTION SPECIALIST

HOW TO...

run faster

This easy-to-follow session from Brentford's strength and conditioning coach, Tom Perryman, will give you an extra yard of pace on the pitch

Safety bar half-squat

Sets: 6 **Reps:** 4

If you are looking to get the better of the opposition full-back in a foot race, then this drill will give you a decent head start. "In football it's very rare to find yourself in a deep squat, so I think a half-squat will translate better for any running and jumping movements while on the pitch," explains Perryman.

Split stance trap bar deadlift

Sets: 6 **Reps:** 4

Rapid speed off the mark will help you to reach through-balls and put defenders on the back foot. "This exercise will develop hip extension power and improve your ability to push off the pitch very quickly and explode away from your opponent."

Single-leg split squat

Sets: 4 **Reps:** 8-10

Kangaroos may well have blistering pace off two feet, but you won't get too far by bounding down the pitch. "To improve speed it's important to enhance single-leg strength. To run efficiently, you also need to be strong enough to hold a sprint position. This routine will enable you to do both."

Single step-up

Sets: 4 **Reps:** 8-10

There's nothing better than watching a speed demon slip through the gears – master this routine and that could soon be you. "This mimics your movement at top speed. Start with one foot an inch above the box, then slam it down and drive up, keeping your hips firm."

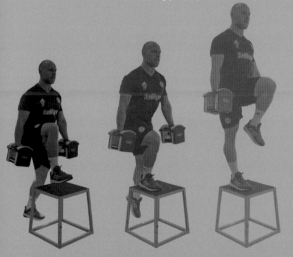

Resisted acceleration drill

Sets: 3 **Reps:** 3

If you don't run with the correct technique you will never fulfil your sprinting potential – but fear not, we're here to help you out. "This is a technical exercise which can have an immediate impact on the pitch. Lean forward and march for 10-15 metres against the resistance, pumping your legs like pistons."

TRAIN LIKE A PRO

The ultimate workouts to get you looking and feeling like a pro

"The squat develops the strength in the lower-body muscles. Combined with jumping exercises, it can increase players' lower-body power output, too"

AFC WIMBLEDON FITNESS COACH
JASON MORIARTY

HOW TO...

fire up your footwork

Make these moves from BXR London coach Courtney Fearon part of your training routine and soon you'll be flummoxing opponents with some lightning-fast feet

1 Tip-toes

Concerned about getting caught on your heels and letting an attacker run through on goal? This move will ensure your feet stay on high alert at all times. "During a match you need to be on your toes so you can change direction swiftly," explains Fearon. "Touch each box with both feet quickly and progress up the ladder."

2 Hip twists

Footballers love showing off their dance skills after scoring a goal. But this isn't the Roger Milla shuffle; it's a quick-fire routine that helps to soup up your soles. "Instead of jumping straight through each box, leap to the left and then to the right, twisting your hips as you move."

3 Back and forth

Intricate footwork will allow you to avoid crunching tackles and evade opponents like a Jack Russell. "This one is all about speed. Put your left foot in the ladder, then spring backwards so that both feet are outside of it, before placing your right foot in the next box. Keep alternating feet until you have reached the end of the ladder."

4 Agility drill

A slippery winger could leave you chasing shadows for 90 minutes – but not if your feet are razor sharp. "Start on the middle cone, then dart sideways to the right cone, dash to the left cone and return to the middle one. Repeat that sequence at high speed for 30 seconds."

5 Medicine ball skater jumps

The simplest of exercises can be the most effective if you're looking to bolt beyond a marker. "Hold a medicine ball and begin by leaping off your right foot and landing on your left. In the same move, jump back to the starting position and repeat for 30 seconds. Using one leg mimics playing football, and adding weight improves power."

ALL EXERCISES 30 SECS 3 SETS

TRAIN LIKE A PRO

The ultimate workouts to get you looking and feeling like a pro

"*Yoga is great preparation for training and aids recovery afterwards. Gareth Southgate did 12 Sun Salutation exercises ahead of each session at Middlesbrough*"

TRAIN LIKE A PRO

The ultimate workouts to get you looking and feeling like a pro

"The forward lunge is a safe and easy move to bolster the legs. It mainly targets quadriceps and glutes but works lower limb muscles as well"

OLLIE HARRINGTON, READING ACADEMY
SPORTS SCIENTIST

HOW TO...

roll away your post-match pain

AFC Wimbledon's first-team fitness coach, Jason Moriarty, has five exercises to speed up your recovery after a game, with a little help from foam rollers

1 Calves

Rolling around on a bit of sponge might look like a laugh, but there's a reason why players often do it straight after a match. "Research has shown muscle soreness peaks at 48 hours if you don't foam roll, but at 24 hours if you do," says Moriarty. "Rolling increases your range of motion so your legs get fresher faster."

2 Quadriceps

Running, twisting and turning causes stiffness in your legs. There's an easy way to give them some much-needed TLC. "Players perform about 54 decelerations in a 90-minute game, which reduces the range of motion of your quads. Rolling them with a long, slow sweeping motion loosens them up."

3 Adductors

Sprinting and whipping crosses into the penalty area will fire up your adductors but can leave them feeling sore. Straddle your roller to sort them out. "Rolling should be done in three portions: just above the knee to work the bottom end of the femur, then the midpoint and finally to the top third near the groin area."

4 Hamstrings

Kicking off your working week with burning hamstrings is no fun. Even worse, damaged hammies can increase the risk of injury. "A full range of motion is vital for performance gains and avoiding physical problems – a firmer foam roller will help to give you better results."

5 Glutes

If you spend your Sunday mornings giving defenders twisted blood, your gluteus medius muscles will take a real hammering. "It's a key area to roll because the glutes directly affect the muscles in your lower back. To do it effectively, roll back and forth in short pulses."

HOW TO... jump higher

Leap like a salmon and dominate the skies thanks to this early-season lower-body workout from strength and conditioning coach Sam Pepys

+ Seated box jump

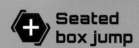

Don't get comfortable – you are not about to get a nice sit-down in the middle of the session. The seated box jump is a power exercise and focuses on jumping at speed. "This replicates your body position in a match when you're leaping for a header and helps the landing phase," explains Pepys.

+ Single-leg step-up

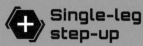

If you want to leap up the steps to get your medal at the end of the season, then get on this nifty move. "Start off by placing your right foot on a box or bench and then leap upwards before landing on both feet. Perform five of these repetitions and switch legs. This will also help your change of direction."

+ Trap bar deadlift

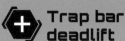

This exercise will super-charge your hamstrings and glutes, and is safer than using a traditional barbell. "The trap bar makes it a lot easier for you to avoid rounding your lower back, which can lead to injury problems."

+ Split squat

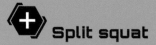

Sprinting into the penalty area and scoring with a towering header requires impressive single-leg strength. "If you feel comfortable performing a double-leg squat, try this out. It'll boost hamstring and quad strength and allow you to leap off one leg."

ALL EXERCISES 4 SETS, 5 REPS

+ Broad jump

The next time you hurdle an advancing goalkeeper and slot the ball into an empty net, you may have this drill to thank. "In football you need to jump horizontally and vertically. The focus on this is speed – jump forwards as fast as you can. Don't use any load as it will slow you down."

HOW TO... sharpen your change of direction

Strength and conditioning coach Sam Pepys runs you through his core workout that will boost your ability to twist and turn at speed

1 Plank walkout
4 x 30 SECONDS

Hopefully you don't spend too much time on your hands and knees on the pitch, but it's a surefire way to strengthen your core. "This is an advanced version of a normal plank," says Pepys. "By putting your hands out in front, you place more stress through the abdominal area."

2 Cable press
3 x 12 REPS EACH SIDE

Having a glistening set of abs isn't enough if you want to bob and weave at speed. "This will work your anterior sling, which is a group of muscles from the groin on one side over to your abdominals on the other. It all needs to work together when you change direction."

3 Frontal pallof hold
3 x 30 SECONDS HOLD EACH SIDE

Sometimes a stepover isn't enough to beat a defender – this'll help you to hold off your marker and dart away. "When you change direction, you are not just moving forwards and backwards. Your core needs to be really strong in different planes and able to resist external force from challenges."

4 Cable wood chop
3 x 12 REPS EACH SIDE

Ever woken up the morning after a game with a sore back, hips or obliques? That's your core's way of telling you that it's not strong enough. "Your core has got to be strong enough to maintain a set position, and express strength as well. Using a cable with a small amount of resistance allows you to train that ability."

5 Medicine ball toss
3 x 6 REPS EACH SIDE

FFT loves nothing more than giving the opposition a shove and then sprinting off before we receive any retribution. You can learn to do the same. "It is important to have enough core strength to apply force at speed – throwing a 3-6kg medicine ball in an explosive fashion improves your power."

TRAIN LIKE A PRO

The ultimate workouts to get you looking and feeling like a pro

"The deadlift is an important exercise for increasing maximal strength. It targets the 'posterior chain' – the lower back, glutes and hamstrings – but will work most of the muscles, too"

PREMIER LEAGUE STRENGTH AND CONDITIONING COACH, MATTHEW WILLMOTT

HOW TO...

boost your balance

Injury prevention expert, Sharon Heidaripour, used this yoga routine with the Arsenal and Chelsea stars – try it for yourself to improve strength and flexibility

Tree pose

Are you no stranger to feeling a decade older when crawling out of bed the day after a game? Make this move a part of your pre-match warm-up. "Footballers will often suffer from stiff hips after years of jumping, kicking and turning on the dominant side," explains Heidaripour. "Hold this position for around 15-20 seconds, then repeat it with your opposite leg to open up your groin and hip."

Standing pigeon

Is it a bird? Is it a plane? Nope, it's a handy yoga pose designed to get your body working in sync. "Football operates in three planes of movement - side to side, up and down, and rotational - and yoga is the same. This will aid your strength, balance, mobility and flexibility."

Half moon pose

If you can master this move, you will soon be able to slalom past defenders without falling flat on your face. Ace. "Ensure you are in perfect alignment, so your arm and leg are in a straight line. This will improve your balance on one leg - which you're going to need for almost every action in a match - as well as activating glute muscles."

Warrior III pose

We don't want any nasty muscle injuries ruining your season, so listen up and add this to your training regime. "This aims to enhance balance and strength on your standing leg and switches on your glutes. Moving your leg forwards and kicking through mimics exactly what happens during a match. It's perfect to do before a game."

Single-leg side plank pose

We have had enough of you making excuses for getting bullied off the ball. This exercise will boost your ability to retain possession and then make a pass. "I used this move a lot with Mesut Özil. It replicated him pushing away an opponent, while lifting his leg in a football-specific fashion helped to strengthen his groin."

train in the rain

Think it's too wet to sharpen your game? Pah! Science says you gain more from working out in stormy weather, and we've got the drills to make the most of the drizzle

SUPER LEGS 1

Build powerful thighs to improve your speed, power and jumping ability. "Perform 20 squats, 20 lunges, 20 scissor squats and 10 jump squats," explains Scott Moody, founder of athletefit.com. "Go immediately from one to the next with no break. The set should take a minute. Take a minute's rest between each set, and repeat three times."

AGILITY HOPS 2

You probably haven't tried hopping since you were 12, but the motion is a great way to improve balance strength and stability. "Do a mixture of forwards and sideways hops, first on the right leg, then the left," says Scott. "Do as many as you can for 15 seconds – two sets. Mix these with five-yard dashes, focusing on quick steps, 90-degree cuts and changes of direction."

GET DRENCHED DOING DRILLS – IT WORKS!

Mankind's desire to avoid freezing to death can stop us from heading outside. But once you overcome that mental obstacle, the same instinct will actually help you work harder.

A study by Japanese researchers published in the *International Journal of Sports Medicine* found that people who trained in low temperatures and rain unsurprisingly worked harder, and burned off more energy, than those who enjoyed pleasant conditions.

Why? Because you're hoodwinking your brain. A cooler environment leads to the perception of less exertion, while the fact that you're staying cool means there's less chance of getting overheated and exhausted.

Like a besuited businessman legging it for a bus in a downpour, there's also the psychological motivation of getting back to nicer conditions, which can push you to complete your exercise faster. And once you're back inside, you can feel the smug glow of a hardcore trainer who is putting in the time when others are huddled indoors. Have a pat on the back. And a bath.

for major gains

WALL PASS AND TURN

4

Many a top pro chiselled their close control with just bricks and mortar. "Do three minutes of work against a wall," says Scott. "Play the ball off the surface and focus on your first touch. When you receive the ball, turn and perform a three-to-five-touch move, as if creating space. Move into the space and play the ball off the wall again." Take a three-minute break, then start the drills again. Go round three or four times.

5yds

BALL CONTROL

3

To get quicker feet you need only a ball and five square yards of grass. "Burst forwards and backwards with the ball," advises Scott, "facing the same way and getting creative with your touch. Do four 30-second sets, resting for 15 seconds in between. Focus on quickness. You can also do this drill laterally, from side to side. The smaller the space, the more demanding the drill."

TRAIN LIKE A PRO

The ultimate workouts to get you looking and feeling like a pro

"Explosive medical ball throws boost power and speed.

HOW TO...

throw a player off the ball

These power moves from strength and conditioning coach Cameron Goff will help you to shrug off the opposition and inspire your team to victory

1 Clean pull
4 sets of 3 reps

Your body works as a chain on the pitch, and you have to train the same way if you want to throw a defender around like a rag doll. "Focus on the triple extension of the ankle, knee and hip," explains Goff. "Your hips should come through the bar, followed by a big shrug and an aggressive calf raise to finish."

CHOOSE 3-4 EXERCISES AND PERFORM TWO WORKOUTS PER WEEK

3 Single leg jumps
4 sets of 4 reps with each leg

If you're running, jumping or barging an opponent, there's every chance you will be doing it on one leg. "This exercise transfers to the pitch perfectly. As you land, explode over the next hurdle as quickly as you can and stay upright throughout. No hurdles? No problem. You can do this without them."

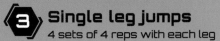

4 Floor press into inverted rows
3 sets of 8-12 reps for each

Dragging and pushing players around the pitch for 90 minutes requires ace upper-body strength and endurance. Perform these two back-to-back with no rest in between. "The floor press is a great alternative to the bench press. The inverted rows will build strength in your upper back and arms."

2 Repeated squat jumps
4 sets of 4 reps

Looking to shove someone and then sprint off in the other direction? This move boosts your explosive strength and jump height. "Start in a half squat position, like you'll often do in a match, and leap as fast and as high as possible. The emphasis here is on speed, so you don't need to use a heavy weight."

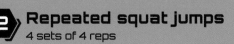

5 Medicine ball throws
3 sets of 5 reps

The manager won't be chuffed if you use a team-mate for shoving practice at training, so grab a medicine ball instead. "Your power should come from your hips and transfer through your shoulders. This is a really good exercise that will improve your ability to throw a player off the ball."

HOW TO...

repair your body

Ease post-season stiffness and strengthen your core for the new season with this session from pilates instructor Benedict Sullivan

1 The 100

Running on rock-hard pitches often leaves your back in tatters, but you can remedy this using one simple move. "Keep your lower back flat on the mat and pull your belly in," explains Sullivan. "Lift up your legs and hold that position. Breathe in for a count of five and breathe out for a count of five. Do it 10 times."

ALL EXERCISES DO 1-3 CIRCUITS WITH NO REST BETWEEN MOVES

3 Double leg stretch

Having the strength to maintain a fixed position while moving at pace helps you to brush past the opposition. You can improve that power by doing this exercise. "Point your arms and legs towards the ceiling, then lower your arms down and around until they're at your sides. That's one rep - do 10-12."

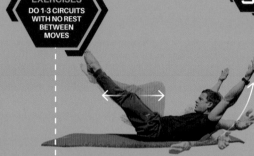

4 Single leg stretch

If you want your body to function in perfect harmony while you're running around the pitch, you need to build a strong core. "Put both hands behind your head and engage your abs. Extend one leg, then do the same on the other side. Moving one side while the other is stationary will test your core."

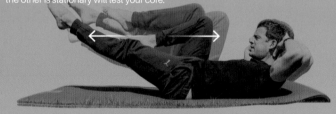

2 Double leg lowers

A strong core will allow you to dart away from an opponent at speed and swivel your hips like Lionel Messi. "Lower both legs down, while keeping your back flat. A lot of people arch their back because they're not strong enough in this area. Don't be one of them."

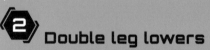

5 Single straight leg stretch

Tight hip flexors and sore hamstrings are common problems among footballers after a hard 90 minutes, but this lower-body move will quickly loosen you up. "Hold your left leg at a 90-degree angle pointing towards the ceiling, then slowly lower the right. Swap legs and repeat."

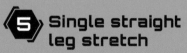

HOW TO...

recover faster

These mobility exercises, recommended by strength and conditioning coach Cameron Goff, will help to relieve your stiffness the day after a match and prepare you for a light training session

Back rocks

If your back has taken a hammering on a hard pitch or from an opposing centre-back, this exercise will help to straighten you out. "Lie on your back and bring your legs into your chest, nice and high," says Goff. "Then you simply rock forwards and backwards, making sure you stay nice and tight throughout."

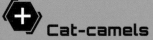

Cat-camels

Goalkeepers and defenders often suffer with bad backs, so we have taken inspiration from the animal world to lengthen and strengthen the spine muscles. "Get on your knees and ensure they stay in line with your shoulders. Then bring your head towards your chest before pulling it up towards the ceiling."

+ Leg extension

Sprinting up and down the wing can take its toll on your legs, so try this to ease those tight hamstrings. "Bring one knee up to your chest - not too far - and then stretch your lower leg towards the ceiling as far as it will go."

+ Back rolls

Changing direction at speed for 90 minutes leaves the hips feeling tender, but this'll loosen you up. "Start in a neutral position and roll your hips to one side. Keep your spine straight and feel a stretch, then repeat the exercise on the other side."

Adductor leg swings

Whipping in crosses or stretching to make blocks can cause hips and groins grief. Relieve tightness with this move. "Start with your leg straight up in the air and then roll it across, 45 degrees, to one side, keeping the other leg straight on the floor."

TRAIN LIKE A PRO

The ultimate workouts to get you looking and feeling like a pro

"Hurdle drills help to develop pace, agility and coordination. They can be made part of pre-match warm-ups and low-grade plyometric circuits, too"

JOHN HARTLEY, ASTON VILLA'S FIRST-TEAM PHYSIO

HOW TO... stay fit between games

Strength and conditioning coach Cameron Goff's interval circuit is designed to maintain your match fitness during the week by keeping your engine running

CIRCUIT 1&2
30 SECS ON + 15 SECS OFF

CIRCUIT 3&4
20 SECS ON + 20 SECS OFF

CIRCUIT 5&6
20 SECS ON + 10 SECS OFF

1 Kettlebell swings

If you're keen to get your heart and lungs burning like they do in a match, then this exercise is an ideal place to start. "Moving resistance at high intensity will really raise your heart rate," reveals Goff. "Make sure you hinge at your hips, as this isn't a squat and swing. Keep it nice and tight, but don't over-arch the back."

3 Weighted dead bug

A robust core enables you to run and turn more efficiently. "This is much better – though a little bit trickier – than a standard sit-up. Make sure you tuck your knees in to get a good squeeze. You should find this one slightly easier on your engine than the previous two exercises, to prepare you for the final two."

4 Reverse lunge

Without a sturdy pair of pins, you'll be unable to sprint box-to-box and make the most of all your fitness work. "This boosts glute activation. Footballers suffer from many hamstring problems – to avoid that you've got to have strong hamstrings and glutes, so this is a great move to help you remain injury-free."

2 Clean and press

This full-body movement ensures that you build a durable engine and strong exterior. "This works hundreds of muscles and is perfect for developing power. Start off at the ground, or mid-shin if you don't think you have the mobility. Drive through the hips before dropping into a front squat and then driving back up to your head."

5 Mountain climbers

Running is a lot more difficult when you are on the floor with your hands in front of you. "Mimicking a running motion as you hold yourself up with your hands is taxing on your engine but also your core. Bring your knees up as high as possible and you will really start to feel it burn, so no cheating right at the end!"

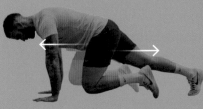

TRAIN LIKE A PRO

The ultimate workouts to get you looking and feeling like a pro

"Good pelvis control and the ability to move both hips independently is a great trait, lowering the risk of injury"

BRENTFORD STRENGTH COACH
TOM PERRYMAN

HOW TO...

brush off your marker

Make these five muscle-building moves from Nike trainer Courtney Fearon part of your workout routine, and soon you'll be throwing players off the ball

+ Pull-up

Sets: 4 **Reps:** 5

To put your muscle to good use around the pitch, first you've got to be able to control your own bodyweight. "Pull-ups are a great exercise for increasing upper-body strength," says Courtney. "If you can't do them, try an assisted pull-up or lat pull-down machine - that will help to build your base strength."

+ Bent over row

Sets: 4 **Reps:** 5

Spending all day hunched over the laptop affects posture and could hinder your performance on the pitch, but this nifty move will soon straighten you out. "It targets the major muscle groups in your back, helping to correct posture and reduce the risk of sustaining injuries in the future."

+ Pallof press

Sets: 4 **Reps:** 10-15

Developing a strong core will enable you to hold off opponents and keep the ball. "Rotate and pull the band or cable towards you until it's just in front of your chest. Then press it out in front of you before slowly bringing it towards your body again. Working against resistance mimics a player trying to pull you back in a match."

+ Push press

Sets: 4 **Reps:** 5

To leap like a salmon and score bullet headers, you will need to pair a strapping upper body with powerful pins. "It's an excellent full-body exercise, working your quads and calves as well as the shoulders and triceps. Being able to transfer force quickly from the lower body to the upper boosts your jumping height over time."

+ Bench press

Sets: 4 **Reps:** 5

If you're jostling for possession with a defender, a robust upper body will allow you to come out on top "A dumbbell press is better than using a bar because it ensures you establish balanced upper-body strength. Doing four sets of five reps will improve your power without making you big like a bodybuilder."

body & mind

Man v Fat football is the six-a-side league in which losing weight is the secret to winning matches. FFT finds out how the programme is helping portly players to enjoy a new lease of life

"great performance, you've just bagged a hat-trick"

Words Alec Fenn **Photography** Tom Clazie Flynn

onight could be Tony Blanc's big night, and he knows it. He's turned up over an hour early for what could be a title-deciding showdown, with his hair slicked back like a mafia boss. If everything goes to plan, his goals will fire his team to glory and seal the first silverware of his career. However, while Tony shares his surname with a World Cup-winning defender, he looks nothing like a footballer. At 28 years old, he weighs 25 stone. And that weight could be the key to victory.

Blanc turns out for 2Lose, a six-a-side team which competes in a Man v Fat league every Tuesday night on an artificial pitch opposite Leyton Orient's Brisbane Road ground. The 14-week competition is designed to help men lose weight, with results influenced not only by events on the pitch, but also the pounds shifted by each team. Bonus goals are awarded to the players who shed timber and then added to the final score, meaning matches are often won or lost on the scales.

Tonight's fixture pits leaders 2Lose against second-placed Blackjack, who trail them by two points. But before the scheduled 7.45pm start, every player must undergo a weigh-in inside a small classroom at the leisure centre next door, normally used to school the Orient academy players. It's the first match since the two-week Christmas break, but Blanc's optimistic about his weight after going easy on the mince pies. "I gave myself Christmas Eve and Christmas Day off, but I didn't want to ruin all my hard work," he tells FFT.

Any weight loss, no matter how small, is rewarded with an extra half a goal, while three successive weeks of successful fat-fighting is called a hat-trick and worth one bonus strike. Hitting long-term targets pays the biggest dividends, and provides an incentive to remain disciplined throughout the season. If a player drops five to 10 per cent of his body weight, his prize is 2.5 goals for the team. This evening, Blanc is set to hit all three targets and score four before he has even set foot on the pitch. "They are the best footballing team in the league, but hopefully if I'm on weight I'll score a few additional goals on the scales and give us a big boost," he explains.

The players are a range of shapes and sizes. There are several tubby 20-somethings, middle-aged blokes with paunches and others – like Blanc – who are at the start of a long road back to physical health. To enrol in the league, men must have a body mass index over 27.5. The BMI measure divides weight in kilograms by height in metres to work out if someone is overweight. These two outfits are far from alone in being out of shape – a further six sides complete their division, while there are another 60 across the UK. More are ready to launch – in both England and Australia – later in the year. Collectively, 6,000 men have shed 64,000 pounds and counting in the space of two years.

"WHEN I LEFT SCHOOL THAT WAS THE END OF PLAYING – UNTIL NOW"

Top Left Players step on the scales before taking to the turf for the crucial top-of-the-table tussle between 2Lose (in red) and Blackjack, with any pounds shed converted into extra goals Bottom left 'Colinho' looked to add some unexpected samba flair to the clash Below Every player fills in a handbook to keep tabs on food intake and track their weight loss

Man v Fat football was born in January 2016, when journalist Andrew Shanahan recognised there was a gap in the market for a weight-loss programme specifically for men. After ballooning to 18 stone, he had found there was next to no support available to men who wanted to lose inches from their waistline. "The whole weight-loss industry was targeted at women," he tells FFT. "I had no confidence and didn't want to join a gym, as I thought I'd have a heart attack. I remember being the only bloke at a Slimming World class. People told me men weren't interested in losing weight, only getting fit, but I didn't really believe it. There are currently 20 million obese men in the UK – they just needed something built for them."

After trialling a Weight Watchers-style event, which he admits was a complete disaster – "for eight weeks there was just me and the vicar who turned up" – he struck gold. Shanahan thought a football-based initiative would appeal to blokes and create an environment in which they would feel more comfortable talking about flab-fighting issues. Each player would be assigned a team and play one 30-minute game per week. Team WhatsApp groups could act as forums for the players to keep each other motivated during the week and build friendships between team-mates. A handbook would enable them to record their food and drink intake each week and track their weight-loss progress, while a fat-fighting coach would weigh all the players and tot up the final scores at the end of the night.

One thousand men applied for 80 spots in the inaugural league, in Solihull, with the 14-week programme proving a resounding success. Ninety-five per cent of players lost weight and 62 per cent managed to shed five per cent of their mass. The average weight lost was two stone. From a solitary league a movement grew, as word spread of an alternative to zumba classes and punishing boot camps. Men who had not kicked a ball in years dragged themselves off their armchairs and ditched the pints for protein shakes. Blanc was one of them. "I hadn't played since I left school," he admits as he steps off the scales, having recorded a weight loss of 0.4kg and bagged four goals. "I was always the biggest so would normally get put in goal, but after I left at 16 that was the end of playing football and any active lifestyle."

One night last year, Tony decided it was time to regain control of his health and his life. "My confidence was really low. Everyone around me had girlfriends, but I was usually the quiet one standing in the corner at parties." He weighed nearly 28 stone, having progressively put on weight after starting his first office job at 18, for the betting company where he still works. "I'd get up, have breakfast and then be sat down for eight hours. Then I'd come home, watch television and go to bed – that was my life." His diet was also killing him. "Fizzy drinks were the big thing for me," he says. "Four times a week I'd go to the pub after work with colleagues and have nine or 10 pints. Then I'd have a can of coke and a big bag of crisps when I got home."

Blanc's first step was to explore the possibility of undergoing gastric band surgery, but he was put off by the £5,000 price. He continued to search for a solution online, scrolling past all the Weight Watchers and Slimming World ads until hearing of Man v Fat and taking the plunge. "I'm a West Ham fan and I've loved football since I was about seven, so it was perfect for me," he adds. "It has been amazing so far. I didn't realise there were so many other people who'd had the same issues as me. Everybody is so supportive and our WhatsApp group has been a great place to chat and share things, which have really helped with our weight loss." He has already shed nearly three stone and noticed a change in mindset. "My confidence has improved and I'm socialising a lot more. It feels great to be able to fit into clothes which I wouldn't have been able to wear six months ago."

Another man who's felt the psychological benefits of losing weight is 42-year-old Blackjack player Graham Farquharson. He stands at 5ft 10in tall but weighs 15st 4lb. His white hair and black-rimmed glasses give him a studious look. "I thought about it for a year before I signed up," he tells FFT. "I was a bit reluctant to begin with. I thought, 'What's everyone else going to be like?' I've had problems with anxiety. I'd feel very overwhelmed before meetings at work and afterwards I'd reward myself for getting through it by having chocolate or a couple of beers. I've cut that crap out and have a smoothie instead now."

"i got down to 18 stone and was loving playing again – it felt great to be scoring goals and getting my fitness back"

Though his weight loss has been slow and steady so far – Graham's dropped eight pounds since joining – football's given him a new lease of life. "My anxiety and mental health has really improved," he reveals. "Doing plenty of exercise, meeting new people and making friends has definitely helped me."

"I HAD HIT 25 STONE AND MY DOCTOR WAS WORRIED"

Glancing around the room, it is difficult to imagine that this evening's encounter will be a competitive affair, but that's a misconception and newcomers are often taken by surprise. "I thought it would be a load of fat blokes wobbling around the pitch," admits Farquharson. "But the skill level is actually pretty high. You can tell that a lot of the guys have played football in the past."

The two sets of players make the short walk from the leisure centre to the artificial pitch, where they're made to wait before warming up while a squad of Orient's academy players conclude their session. The contrast between the two groups of males could hardly be greater, but while their build and ability is considerably different, they all share the same competitive drive to win. Weight loss is the number one goal, but this is a game of football and there is a Man v Fat league title at stake.

Before kick-off, the 2Lose players gather in a huddle to discuss their strategy. One member claims they've got the pace to catch Blackjack by surprise on the break, but the blank expressions of his team-mates suggest they don't share his admirable optimism. Their approach will be to sit deep and stay compact, with Blanc an imposing presence at the back, and attack when an opportunity arises. At first glance their opponents appear more physically able and their confidence is evident in some of the names printed on the reverse of their shirts. Randall has opted for the moniker 'Fk N Ell', while the nickname of his team-mate 'Colinho' suggests he may be able to offer some unlikely samba flair, despite his large frame.

As the top-of-the-table match gets underway, it seems like a good time to talk to the league's coach, Doug Curtis, whose own story offers a reminder that weight loss can be a long road riddled with setbacks. Curtis learned about Man v Fat football while he wolfed down another fat-laden meal in front of *The One Show* with his family in May 2016. "I had just hit 25 stone and my doctor informed me I had high blood pressure," he tells *FFT*. "I was also borderline diabetic, so I knew I had to change something before it was too late."

Seven years of night shifts as a retail worker had wreaked havoc with his sleep pattern and made him extremely vulnerable to the late-night temptations of vending machines. "I became lazy," he says. "I'd often have four meals a day: breakfast, lunch, dinner and then another meal at around 1am. Then I would eat first thing in the morning and go to bed. I was scoffing sausage rolls, fatty sandwiches, chocolate, crisps and fizzy drinks – basically everything a human shouldn't be eating." He joined a gym and managed to shift several stone before signing up for Man v Fat football, and his weight has continued to plummet. "I've cut out all of the bad food, started eating fruit and vegetables and got myself down to 18 stone. I was loving playing football again. I stopped playing regularly at 23, so it felt great to be scoring goals every week and getting my fitness back."

Unfortunately, an operation on a double hernia slammed the brakes on his weight loss before he was struck down by Lyme disease upon his return, after being bitten by a tick during a match.

His ill-health has forced him to swap playing for an admin role while he recovers, and it's also seen him pile the pounds back on. "I've found it really hard," he concedes. "I've put on four stone, but I'm hoping to start playing again from next season and get back down to 18 stone. That's my long-term target."

"I DON'T WANT TO BE THE FAT DAD. I WANT TO RUN AROUND THE PARK"

Back on the pitch, the first half is an even affair, played at a surprising intensity, as the teams go toe-to-toe. Several timely interceptions and simple passes earn Blanc the applause of his team-mates, but midway through the opening period there's nothing the formidable enforcer can do as Blackjack take the lead. It's a big blow to the league leaders, but there's a reason 2Lose are top dogs and they quickly respond with an equaliser to make it 1-1 at the break.

The next 15 minutes could decide the title and Blackjack's superior fitness begins to show, while Blanc is forced to come off briefly after stumbling and crashing to the floor following a defensive header. His team-mates appear equally dazed as Randall begins to run riot, with his second half hat-trick helping to fire his side to a 6-1 win. It means 2Lose must hope they've performed better on the scales to claw back the scoreline and stay in top spot.

As the teams walk off, there's an unexpected warmth and etiquette between the blokes as they exchange bear hugs and compliment each other on their respective performances. After another hard half-hour, they're all another week closer to achieving their targets.

"I'm going to be playing for a long time," says Blanc. "I haven't set myself a number, it's about slowly chipping away at my weight."

Farquharson is hoping his weight loss will have an impact at home. "I've got two daughters, who are six and 11," he says. "I don't want to be the fat dad. I want to be able to run around the park with them and set a good example – if I can get down to 90kg I'll be happy."

Randall's goals are a bit more short-term. "I've made a lot of mates here. It will be great to go out for a curry and a few beers at the end of the season – or should I say a slimline G and T?!"

Twenty-four hours later, a WhatsApp message from Curtis informs both teams that, despite Blanc's valiant effort on the scales, the final score is 2Lose 5-6 Blackjack, leaving three teams level on points at the summit. Next week the same portly chaps will return to the scales and do battle under the lights, although they're all on the same side, really. This is Man v Fat, after all.

THE
secret

Football is leaving no mattress unturned in its quest for the perfect night's kip. Sleep gurus, napping pods and wearable tech help today's stars to stay fit and firing in ways their predecessors wouldn't have dreamt of

here was a time when sleep was just the thing superstar footballers squeezed in between boozy nights down the pub and turning up to training the next morning. As George Best quipped, "I've stopped drinking, but only while I'm asleep."

But that all changed when a letter from a Slumberland salesman landed on Alex Ferguson's desk in the mid-90s. Nick Littlehales asked if the Manchester United manager had thought about the impact a good night's kip could have on the performance of his players. Intrigued, Fergie invited Littlehales to The Cliff to deliver a presentation to him and his squad.

Gary Pallister listened with particular interest. His back was in such a state that seats had been removed from the team coach to allow him to lie on a mattress on the way to away matches. Littlehales, determined to get to the bottom of Pally's pain, paid a visit to the defender's home, where he discovered that the United star had been sleeping on a rock-hard Bensons mattress. He swiftly swapped it for something a little softer on Pallister's 6ft 4in frame, and also provided him with suitable pillows to keep his posture aligned while he slept.

Littlehales immediately had a raft of new customers. Within weeks, he had kitted out the houses of Ferguson and Ryan Giggs with similar snooze-improving setups. Word spread throughout football, and soon he was sending a Transit van full of suitable duvets and pillows to a hotel in France, to help David Beckham & Co. sleep more soundly during England's 1998 World Cup campaign. Newspapers got wind of Littlehales' work, and overnight he became football's first sleep coach – all while still flogging mattresses from an office in Oldham.

SCIENCE OF SLEEP

Words Alec Fenn

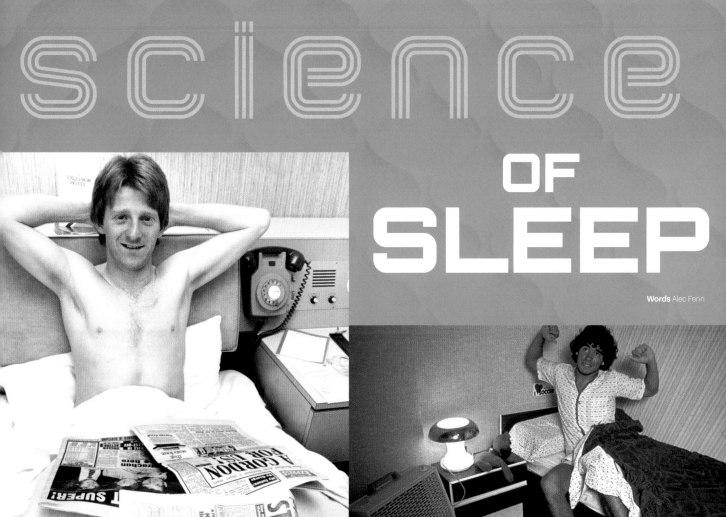

Having put his long-held ambition to open a furniture shop on hold, Littlehales set off travelling the world to educate some of the world's biggest sports teams on the impact of sleep on performance. A talk at Arsenal captivated Thierry Henry and Gunners physio Gary Lewin, who put in a good word with England manager Sven-Goran Eriksson.

Before long, Littlehales was inspecting every bedroom at England's Euro 2004 training base in Lisbon and creating individual sleep profiles for each player, finding out everything about their lifestyle, diet and bedtime routine, and advising them accordingly. His reputation grew, and a similar gig with Team GB's cycling team followed.

These days, the game's top sides are well aware of the crucial edge their players can gain by getting the best sleep possible. Real Madrid, Manchester City, Liverpool and Tottenham have all sought advice from Littlehales and a growing number of experts in the science of sleep, while Southampton, Bournemouth and Brentford are using the latest wearable tech to monitor and improve their players' rest.

zzZ

In American sports, where teams often travel through multiple time zones for fixtures, getting adequate shut-eye is essential. In 2016, Cheri Mah, who specialises in sleep and performance in NBA, NFL and MLB stars, was recruited by ESPN to work on their 'Schedule Alert' project. She created a sleep formula to predict when NBA teams would lose, dependent on how far they had to travel between games. She identified 42 matches in which she believed clubs were at risk of fatigue-related defeat, and correctly predicted the outcome of 29. The next season, her hit rate was a staggering 42 from 54.

Five years earlier, Mah had conducted a groundbreaking study on a team of college basketball players at Stanford University. It revealed that those who had upped their sleep by an average of 110 minutes, so they slept for 8-10 hours per night, boosted their

shot accuracy by nine per cent and improved their time on a 282-foot sprint drill by 0.7 seconds. It was an improvement in performance comparable with the effects of doping – except it was legal.

The results sent ripples across the Atlantic. Inside Southampton's renowned Black Box – the room where staff dig through mountains of data to inform decisions made on everything from managerial and player recruitment to gym regimes – the club's head of sports science, Alek Gross, got to work. At the behest of gaffer Mauricio Pochettino, he uncovered further research finding that just a single night of bad sleep was enough to weaken a player's immune system and increase the risk of injury. Sleep deprivation lasting beyond 64 hours reduced strength and power and also impaired balance, enhancing the chance of sprains. A rise in the hormone cortisol, prompted by a lack of sleep, could even cause the body to begin eating into its own muscle stores and heighten the possibility of strains and tears.

The alarming findings offered a tantalising opportunity to improve performance, backed up not by mattress sales spin but by science.

Every morning, each Saints player has to rate their previous night's sleep out of 10, using an app's wellbeing questionnaire. If their rating keeps falling below a safe threshold, staff monitor them with wearable tech. Players also have a list of prohibited foods and drinks that they are warned against consuming in the evening. Caffeine and sugary liquids are off the menu, as are fat-laden meals, which take longer to digest and raise body temperature, slowing the process of falling asleep. All players are given a milk-based protein drink to aid recovery and induce sleepiness. "Some players have individual sleep kits to help them during the week, including a duvet and pillow of a specific thickness, and blackout curtains if they need them," says Gross.

Fatigue was a major concern for Mexico's World Cup coach, Juan Carlos Osorio. The majority of his squad had to travel 6,200 miles from Mexico to their Russian base, before flying a combined 3,554 miles for their group games in Moscow, Rostov and Yekaterinburg. He spoke to Ferguson, who introduced him to Man United sports scientist Robin Thorpe, and together they plotted a sleep regime.

Bespoke mattresses for each player were flown to Russia, and the bedrooms were set at a comfortable 18 degrees to help players drift off. Their training schedule was adapted to cater for ideal sleeping times, while players were advised not to use their mobile phones less than an hour before bed. The blue light emitted from such devices can prevent the production of a hormone called melatonin, essential for entering deep sleep and recovery. A post-game cherry-based drink was introduced for its sleep-inducing properties.

Mexico's squad bought into the approach. Indeed, their 38-year-old captain, Rafael Marquez, emerged from the team's hotel before 10pm on the eve of their group-stage clash with South Korea to ask their rowdy fans to keep the noise down, so that they could get some sleep. Hundreds of fans had gathered to sing, chant and hail their heroes, with a mariachi band playing classic Mexican ballads. Getting an early night paid off: El Tri won the game 2-1 and eventually finished ahead of Germany in Group F.

The likes of Marquez, Javier Hernandez and Carlos Vela weren't the only players at this year's World Cup who were taking their sleep seriously.

Switzerland and Arsenal midfielder Granit Xhaka (left) volunteered to be a guinea pig for his sponsor, Under Armour, by test-driving their new range of sleep products. Before he left London, the Gunners midfielder's house was fitted with hi-tech, slumber-friendly lightbulbs and a brand new mattress, while he was also given special glasses that allowed him to look at electronic devices without his eyes being hit with stimulating blue light.

At bedtime, Xhaka slipped into something a little more comfortable: a $200 set of pyjamas, and sheets with ceramic woven into the fabric to regulate his body temperature. He also used a sound-blocking device to ensure he wasn't woken from his slumber, and a sleep monitor recorded the quality of his kip. His habits rubbed off on his Swiss room-mate, Ricardo Rodriguez, who borrowed a pair of his sleep specs during the World Cup.

"an extra 110 minutes of sleep boosted basketball players' speed and shot accuracy to an extent comparable with doping"

zZZ

Yet being back home, tucked up in a king-size four-poster, doesn't guarantee that a footballer will sleep like a log. Sergio Aguero's stocky frame and thick thighs were keeping him awake, until Manchester City called Littlehales in 2014 to ask for the Pallister treatment.

"Aguero was struggling to put his thighs together when he slept on one side, and thought it could be the cause of his hamstring injuries," Littlehales tells *FFT*. "His body position was wrong when he went to bed, which was affecting his sleep."

There was a second problem: "His bed was a fancy leather thing but the mattress was crap." Littlehales prescribed a slimmer type, designed for his height and weight, and thinner pillows, which aligned his neck and spine.

Littlehales realised Aguero's fitful sleep was also the product of living a South American lifestyle in Manchester. "The temperature in his property was 16 to 18 degrees at all times," he explains. "That's perfect for nodding off, but he often wasn't eating until about 11pm at night, which is normal in Argentina and Spain but not ideal when you have to be up for training first thing in the morning,"

Furthermore, genetics were responsible for the striker's hatred of early starts. "Every human has a specific chronotype, which means they're either a morning or a night person; an owl or a lark," adds Littlehales. "Aguero hates early mornings and would rather train in the afternoon if he had the choice." A 90-minute mid-afternoon nap helped the striker to catch up on his Zs and reduced the pressure on him to cram all of his rest into one sleep window. A week after linking up with Littlehales, Aguero scored four goals against Spurs.

Another client at Manchester City was James Milner (below), who was finding it difficult to switch off after Champions League games. "James would play at 7.45pm and not get back until about 1am, and he'd still be wired from the game," says Littlehales. "He would end up staying downstairs, playing on his Xbox until the early hours. He'd get towards feeling knackered enough and fall asleep on the sofa or go to bed. There'd be no training the following day, so he'd be waking up mid-morning, which meant he was completely out of sync."

The solution was to move his sleep time to 2am on Champions League nights and to stick to his usual 6.30am rise. "Humans sleep in cycles of 90 minutes, so he was getting three in before he woke up. If he was still tired, he could top up with a nap between either 1pm and 3pm or 5pm and 7pm, when the body's energy levels dip. This made sure he wasn't fatigued, and also kept to his normal wake-up routine."

Investing in resting is also helping smaller clubs to sleep their way to the top. Last season, Bournemouth gaffer Eddie Howe asked Dr Rob Daniel for help. "Sleep is such an underrated recovery tool," said Howe. "We have all been given sleep specs to wear for bed – I've been wearing them and it helped me sleep better."

Brentford, with one of the smallest budgets in the Championship, linked up with American company Whoop, who supply cutting-edge wrist trackers to professional athletes to measure sleep quality. "Our philosophy is maximising what we do in areas which can give us big gains, and sleep is one of them," the club's head of performance, Chris Haslam, tells *FFT*. "Players are more compliant in training, analysis sessions and gym sessions. They're sharper; they're brighter. And if you do that over a period of time, you develop them in a better way than those who aren't getting the necessary rest and recovery."

zZZ

Attitudes towards sleep are steadily changing in sport. Paul Winsper, Under Armour's vice-president for athlete performance, used to work for several Premier League clubs and has outlined the rationale behind the brand's experiment with Xhaka.

"We treat our athletes like patients," he revealed. "We're educating them about the importance of having a regular bedtime. They need to understand that recovery is just as important as their training."

Littlehales believes that Raheem Sterling's request to be rested on international duty three years ago was a big moment for the sleep movement. "He told Roy Hodgson that he was knackered and people criticised him for that, but people are now beginning to realise the impact of sleep on performance," he explains. "Being tired and getting by on only six hours' sleep used to be a badge of honour, but we have studies that show the dangers of sleep deprivation. Players have to be educated on that. It's OK to be tired, but let's try to fix it."

Under Garry Monk, Swansea introduced 30 inflatable napping pods for players to snooze in between double sessions, and sleep was a key consideration during construction of Man City's cutting-edge training facility. Their 32 ensuite bedrooms were decorated with light green wallpaper featuring ever-decreasing circles, designed to help players drift off. Mattress firm Simba made an aeroplane seat/bed hybrid to help Gareth Bale kip on the 35 flights he averages each year. Various tools let him adjust position to ease pressure on his spine and monitor noise, temperature, light, humidity and air particles.

For the converted, it's paying off. "My sleep is more intense and a lot deeper," said Xhaka, already reaping the benefits. "I've noticed that I now wake up a lot calmer, and I don't use my phone until I leave the house in the morning." At the World Cup, he scored a superb goal in a 2-1 win over Serbia as Switzerland reached the last 16. Mexico also impressed before being knocked out in the same round by Brazil. Bournemouth secured a fourth consecutive season of Premier League football, ending 2017-18 in 12th, while Brentford punched above their financial weight with a 9th-placed finish. Bale's campaign concluded by scoring twice in Madrid's Champions League final win against a Liverpool side featuring Milner, who made 47 appearances in all competitions.

As for Pallister, his new Slumberland mattress didn't, in fact, cure his dodgy back. But at least he slept soundly on it.

pro tips and advïce

IF YOU'RE
GOING TO
DO ONE
THING...

Unplug and switch off

FFT loves nothing more than spending our winter nights tucked up in bed, spooning a football while watching goal compilations on DVD.

But our quality time beneath a Roy of the Rovers duvet could be coming to an end, as a new report reveals that technology might be damaging our sleep.

Researchers at King's College in London and Cardiff University in the Welsh capital analysed 11 studies, involving more than 125,000 people, to determine if electronic devices affect our rest. They discovered that if you use a smartphone or tablet before hitting the sack, or even watch a bit of television, it doubled the risk of you having a bad night's kip - which is the last thing that we want before a match.

And, more worryingly for FFT, the odds remained exactly the same even if the devices were in the bedroom and switched off.

"Our findings are further proof of the detrimental affect media devices have on sleep duration, as well as quality of sleep," said Dr Ben Carter of King's College. Fine, we'll stop watching our DVDs. But no one's going to stop us from playing a quick game of Subbuteo before lights out, OK?

Words Alec Fenn; **Illustration** Alex Williamson

KINESIOLOGY TAPE

Gareth Bale and Mario Balotelli have both been known to like a bit of the blue stuff. The duo, plus many other footballers, have been pictured with kinesio tape stuck to various parts of their body. Created by the Japanese chiropractor Dr Kenso Kase in 1979, it promises to reduce muscular pain, while providing support for joints. Yet, the benefits of the tape may be more psychological than physical. A review by Roger Kerry, an associate professor in the School of Health Sciences at the University of Nottingham, scrutinised various studies into the tape over the last decade and found that it offered minimal performance benefits. We'll just stick to cans of Deep Heat, thanks.

1 "Kinesio-taping a joint can lower the chance of getting an ankle sprain by 51 per cent," explains Michael Callaghan, who was a physio at Everton.

2 "It can also have an impact on the brain in terms of joint position sense, but doesn't have any additional benefits to standard bandaging."

3 "Some suggest kinesio tape will reduce the amount of pain and swelling, but sellotape or gaffer tape have the same effect."

VS

Coloured and patterned tape has become trendy in top-level football, but which is best for avoiding injuries?

DYNAMIC TAPE

It looks like Maori-inspired wallpaper, but there's a reason the likes of Dele Alli and Tim Cahill have started using dynamic tape to ease aches and pains. The trendy-looking strapping provides resistance while lowering the amount of load that gets absorbed through the relevant area, reducing wear and tear on a player's body. Sounds great, but does it really work? Well, a study from the University of Sevilla two years ago analysed the impact of dynamic tape on a footballer with splayed feet. The results found the bandage helped to correct his running gait within 10 days of use and reduced previously painful symptoms. In that case, *FFT* is going to mummify ourselves in the stuff.

1 "This tape is highly elastic so a player's range of movement is not affected with it on," says registered massage therapist Sarah Whiston.

2 "As the muscle or joint lengthens, so does the dynamic tape. This helps to absorb the load of the movement – a bit like a bungee cord."

3 "I've had success using it for both athletic and everyday physical problems, so people can play despite not being 100 per cent."

AND OUR WINNER IS... **DYNAMIC TAPE**

Double your five a day

If your idea of healthy eating is a low-calorie McDonalds meal washed down with some orange juice, we've got bad news.

Researchers at Imperial College London believe the recommended consumption of fruit and vegetables should be raised, so your five a day goes up to a whopping 10.

A study concluded that eating 800 grams of fruit and veg daily lowered the possibility of a stroke by a third and heart problems by 24 per cent.

Lead author Doctor Dagfinn Aune, from the School of Public Health at the university, said: "We wanted to investigate how much fruit and veg you need to eat to gain maximum protection against diseases.

"Eating five portions of fruit and vegetables a day is good, but 10 is better. Fruit and vegetables have been shown to lower cholesterol levels and blood pressure, as well as improve the health of the blood vessels and immune system."

The study also claimed that close to eight million premature deaths could be prevented if people start to follow the new guidelines.

Just think, it could even help you to prolong your playing career.

Words Alec Fenn; **Illustration** Alex Williamson

MEDICINE BALLS

The use of medicine balls dates back 3,000 years when wrestlers in Persia would train with sand-filled bladders. Thankfully, modern versions are not quite so primitive and can be used to build strength, improve jump height and burn calories when used as part of a full-body workout. A study by the

Journal of Strength and Conditioning investigated what effects a 12-week schedule had on the core strength of 49 baseball players. The results found the programme improved abdominal power by more than 18 per cent. Add it to your training regime and you'll be able to twist and turn past defenders and show off a killer six-pack to boot. Sounds like a summer well spent to us.

1 "Medicine balls are great for using with a team-mate in partner throws, plus twist and turn exercises," stated trainer Alonzo Wilson.

2 "If you're looking for a good cardio workout, medicine ball slams will help to raise your heart rate, while also taxing your core."

3 "With resistance machines you're stuck in the same place – a medicine ball offers you the freedom to run, jump, throw and slam it."

VS

Want to build strength and torch calories? These gym favourites will do the trick, but which one's the best?

KETTLEBELLS

Kettlebells were introduced by circus strongmen back in the 19th century. Some of the signature moves include the swing, snatch and clean and jerk, all of which engage your whole body and boost your ability to achieve full movements, like throwing opponents off the ball. They are great for losing weight, too. According to research by the American Council of Exercise, the average person can burn 400 calories during a 20-minute kettlebell routine. That's 20 calories per minute and the equivalent of being able to run a mile in six minutes. So if you are trying to shed some timber and fast-track your fitness ahead of pre-season training, kettlebells could come to your rescue.

1 "The weight is offset from the handle, so it works against you and tests both coordination and strength," explained fitness guru Jamie Lloyd.

2 "About 600 of your muscles will be put to use during a standard session, and that makes kettlebells the ideal tool for a full-body workout."

3 "Kettlebells can vary from 4kg to 48kg in weight, so they can be used by people with different levels of ability and experience."

AND OUR WINNER IS... KETTLEBELLS

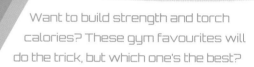

Sip on salt

If you've ever woken up in the middle of the night, wailing in agony with cramp holding onto you in a vice-like grip, a lack of general fitness may not be the reason for your woes.

A study by *Sports Health* found that dehydration and loss of salt during exercise was a main cause of muscle cramping, after a review of research on the topic spanning at least half a century.

Indeed, the Liverpool midfielder Adam Lallana used to suffer from this very problem while he was at Southampton until the south-coast side finally got to the bottom of it.

"We would measure his salt loss during matches and found he was a salty sweater," says their director of sports medicine and science, Mo Gimpel. "Adam was losing a lot of salt, which meant that his muscles were often cramping up."

The solution? The club decided to sprinkle a small amount of salt into a drink he could sip on throughout games, freeing him from his misery.

Try it, but if that doesn't work, you might just be plain unfit.

Words Alec Fenn; Illustration Alex Williamson

CHOCOLATE MILK

Working out would be a lot more fun if we could down a pint of lager after a workout, wouldn't it? Well, modern science is unlikely to suggest we do that anytime soon. However, several experts have backed chocolate milk as a suitable recovery drink. A 2012 study published in the *Medicine and*

Sport Journal revealed a low-fat version of this tasty treat contains a 4:1 carbohydrate to protein ratio. This is the same composition found in many recovery drinks. The same study also found it to be very high in sodium, which aids recuperation. They advised consuming it within two hours of exercise to replenish the body's glycogen stores. Lovely.

ONLY 1.5% fat NO artificial flavours or colours

YAZOO CHOCOLATE MILK SHAKE

1 "Chocolate milk is cheaper than many branded recovery drinks, but the ingredients can be of poor quality," says nutritionist Liam Holmes.

2 "The sugar found inside the drink is cane sugar, instead of a natural source, which means that it has very low nutritional benefit."

3 "If you have done a light run, there is no need for a high-carb drink like this one, as you will not have exhausted all of your carb stores."

VS

ION4 ADVANCED ELECTROLYTE SYSTEM
POWERADE
SPORTS DRINK & VITAMINS B3, B6 & B12
TEXT "PA2010" TO 878787 FOR A CHANCE TO WIN 1 OF 500 COMPLETE ION4® SOCCER PACKS
ORANGE FLAVOR + OTHER NATURAL FLAVORS
32 FL OZ (1 QT) 946 mL

FFT is never sure what to glug after a gruelling 90-minute workout, so we found out how we should refill our system

SPORTS DRINKS

FFT has always been old fashioned and opted for orange squash in favour of the luminous-coloured sports drinks, but it turns out our choice of liquid refreshment may be hampering performance levels. The registered dietician and sports nutritionist, Wendy Martinson, said:

"Water is sufficient for short sessions, but for exercise lasting 60 minutes, an isotonic sports drink is recommended." A study inside the *Journal of Applied Physiology* also learned that taking an isotonic drink before and during any exercise increased treadmill running time to exhaustion by 27 per cent in recreational runners. That'll explain why we run out of gas by half-time!

1 "Sports drinks will all contain electrolytes – potassium and sodium – which are essential for recovery after exercise," adds nutritionist Holmes.

2 "However, be careful to avoid any sports drinks which are entirely glucose-based. Choose something with a mix of carbs as well as protein."

3 "Coconut water is also a good alternative to sports drinks – it contains electrolytes on top of natural sugars."

AND OUR WINNER IS...   **SPORTS DRINKS**

IF YOU'RE GOING TO DO ONE THING...

Put your weak foot forward

Unless you're a Sunday League Santi Cazorla, your weaker foot is probably useless for anything other than standing on.

But AFC Wimbledon's academy have devised a clever method to make players two-footed.

Their starlets have been donning odd socks, and it's not because the kitman keeps getting muddled up. Players wear an odd white sock at training and a yellow one in games, identifying the weak foot.

Opposing players then make them use their weak side and improve the ability with both feet. Once a coach is satisfied a player is ambidextrous, he gets a prize... a second blue sock.

Academy coach, Jeremy Sauer tells *FFT*: "A player can't access all of the decisions available in a game if he is not able to utilise his weaker foot to a competent level."

The scheme is being seen as too obvious by several sceptical clubs, but Sauer is convinced their sock smarts are now paying off.

"Our under-12 lads moving into 11-a-side games now don't think twice before using their weaker foot – it's become a habit."

So, next time you're doing your laundry, remember that it could help you out on the pitch.

Words Alec Fenn Illustration Alex Williamson

SALMON

Vitamin boost

Its bright and healthy complexion means there's no surprise in hearing that salmon is brimming with benefits. Just 200g will give you more than your recommended daily allowance of vitamins B6 and B12, which help your body to release energy from the other foods you eat, so that you can extract every single ounce of goodness from your diet to fuel your performance. Scientists even believe that eating this ocean-dweller could have big mental health advantages. Researchers at Ohio State University found that 2.5g of omega-3 – that's around 12-15 ounces of salmon – eased symptoms of anxiety by some 20 per cent. You won't worry about that goal drought of yours ever again.

1 "In a 100g portion of salmon there is 20g of protein, making it a great muscle-builder," explains nutritionist Jo Scott-Dalgleish.

2 "You'll find roughly 200 calories within a typical serving, which is only about eight per cent of your recommended daily calorie allowance."

3 "Salmon is perfect recovery food after training sessions because of its anti-inflammatory properties, which help to reduce muscle soreness."

It's a seafood derby this month as two protein-packed fishes go head-to-head for nutritional supremacy. If only Andre Marriner had been available to referee...

TUNA

Protein punch

It's becoming fashionable following a workout to shake your protein flask like a cocktail waitress making a dry martini in a James Bond movie, but did you know that there's a cheaper, natural alternative? Your 54p tin of Asda Smart Price tuna won't exactly scream 'gym hipster', but remember that you will get a whopping 40g of protein in a 160g serving – that's more than you will get from two scoops of whey protein picked up in a bodybuilding shop. This makes tuna the perfect fuel to repair your muscles after a match, or to give you Roberto Carlos-sized thighs after a leg session at the gym. And one more thing: the American Heart Association claims that two portions of tuna per week can help to improve heart health. So what's not to like?

1 "There's 6g of fat in every 100g of tuna compared to 13g in the same amount of salmon, making it a leaner fish," says Scott-Dalgleish.

2 "If you're eating tuna, make sure that you eat the fresh variety, as the tinned version will contain far less omega-3."

3 "I'd recommend eating tuna on a day-to-day basis, but to maximize recovery after both training and games, pick salmon."

AND OUR WINNER IS... SALMON

IF YOU'RE GOING TO DO ONE THING...

Lift light

There are few things better for the male ego than throwing your bodyweight in metal around a gym for 10 vein-popping reps, before admiring your taut muscles in the mirror. Don't pretend it's just us...

But what if we've been getting this whole muscle-building thing all wrong? What if lifting lighter weights has always been just as effective as hauling dumbbells the size of small children?

Stuart Phillips, a professor of kinesiology at McMaster University in Ontario, Canada, conducted a study in which one group of men performed a series of exercises using light resistance for 25 reps, while another did the same exercises but with heavy weights for 10 reps.

The results showed both groups made near-identical improvements in muscle size and strength, which, according to Phillips, could be great news for your displays on the pitch.

"Some people are intimidated by lifting heavy weights," he said. "These findings may make people feel more comfortable about commencing a weight training programme. We're also looking into whether lifting lighter weights could help to prevent injuries."

So, if you're a Sunday League sicknote or built like a teenage Luke Chadwick, you may now have the answer to your problem.

Words Alec Fenn

COCONUT OIL

The clean-eating brigade have long highlighted the benefits of cooking using coconut oil, but is it the key to better health or simply another fad? The so-called superfood is higher in saturated fat than butter – however, it contains medium chain fatty acids, which can increase the levels of good cholesterol in the body. Coconut oil also has a relatively high smoke point (177 degrees), meaning it won't begin to burn and release free radicals while you cook. And best of all, it could aid weight loss: a study in the *American Journal of Nutrition* found it boosted the number of calories burnt at rest by 28 women who'd supplemented their diet with the oil for four weeks.

1 "Several studies have hailed the weight loss benefits of coconut oil – but they're too small to be significant," dietitian Louise Robertson said.

2 "Other studies have examined if it could reduce cholesterol levels, but it's high in saturated fat so using lots of it will have a negative effect."

3 "Coconut oil can be pretty expensive to buy, compared with olive and rapeseed oil. Both of these alternatives are just as good for cooking with."

100% raw, cold pressed

the groovy food COMPANY

organic extra virg coconu oil

fry, bake, roast, spread

VS

FFT would rather not use lard while we are cooking up a stir fry, so we put two of the healthiest cooking oils to the test

AVOCADO OIL

As if avocados have not had enough nutritional limelight, the oil extracted from the fruit is now being lauded for its supreme health qualities. It's got a monounsaturated fatty acid level of 74 per cent – this makes it one of the healthiest variants of fat that we can consume, which can reduce the risk of heart disease. Avocado oil is also awash with anti-oxidants, like vitamin E and lutein, that'll help you to reduce cell damage. According to a 2005 study in *Medline*, adding the oil to a salad with carrots, spinach and lettuce raised the absorption of plant pigments. These give fruit and vegetables their bright colours and provide protective health benefits.

1 "Avocado oil is great for cooking with and it can also be a dressing for some uncooked items such as salad and dips," stated Doctor Josh Axe.

2 "Monounsaturated fats found in the oil can also have a beneficial effect on blood pressure – and hence the heart – if eaten in moderation."

3 "It can also help to ease some of the symptoms of itchy skin condition psoriasis, which is more common among older people."

Spectrum NATURALS®

COLD PRESSED

Avocado OIL

AND OUR WINNER IS...   **AVOCADO OIL**

IF YOU'RE GOING TO DO ONE THING...

Detox your ego

Are you that guy who goes for glory from an impossible angle rather than passing when your team-mate is completely free in the six-yard box? Well, the next time you spank the ball over the crossbar, we're going to tell you to detox your ego.

Don't worry, we're not talking about flushing toxins out of your system with a kale smoothie. We mean it's time you learnt how to put the team's interests in front of your own. This is the message that sports psychologist Steven Sylvester is preaching in his book *Detox Your Ego* to help players to fulfill their potential.

"Being selfish out on the pitch is a disastrous mindset," he tells *FFT*. "We want players making the right decisions under pressure and then thinking about how they benefit the team. Serving a higher purpose can help a player to perform to his best."

Still sceptical? Wimbledon striker Lyle Taylor teamed up with Steven last term and scored 23 goals as the Dons won promotion to League One.

So, try detoxing your ego and you and your team-mates could soon be reaping the rewards.

Words Alec Fenn; Illustration Alex Williamson

QUINOA

These days you can't scroll through your Instagram feed without seeing a picture of a so-called superfood that is dressed up to the nines in an exotic dressing. Quinoa is now a favourite among social media health fanatics, but what exactly is all the fuss about? This nutritious crop has been grown in South America for thousands of years and belongs to the same nutritional family as beets, chard and spinach. Quinoa is considered a far superior alternative to starchy carbs such as bulgur wheat, rice and couscous because of its high protein content, which is perfect for repairing your body after training, a rigorous 90 minutes or working out in the gym.

1 "Quinoa contains 14g of protein per 100g," says nutritionist Gavin Allinson, "plus amino acids, which you need to repair your muscles."

2 "It's a very versatile food, because you can serve quinoa with vegetables as part of a salad, or alternatively alongside meat or fish."

3 "It's a great option to have during the off-season or on a rest day as it contains lower carbohydrate content than rice and pasta."

VS

We love our carbohydrates at FFT – but which type should we be eating to fuel our performance?

RICE

You just can't beat a good serving of rice with a nice takeaway, can you? Unfortunately a chicken tikka masala probably isn't the ideal fuel for a game on a Saturday. However, rice is a staple food for more than half of the world's population, particularly in Asia, and is cultivated in excess of 100 countries.

The brown variety can also provide a steady release of carbohydrates – ensuring you stay fuller for longer, meaning you won't crave sugary foods which could derail your New Year health kick. Arsenal's players even eat sushi – which consists of vinegared rice and seafood – after their matches. If it's good enough for Arsene's boys, it'll do for you.

1 "Just 7g of protein is contained in every 100g of rice – so that's exactly half the amount that's found in 100g of quinoa," says Allinson.

2 "White rice can be broken down into glucose quickly. It's an ideal way of restoring carbohydrate stores in the body after training."

3 "There's no need to eat rice other than after matches as quinoa will provide you with carbohydrates and high nutritional value."

AND OUR WINNER IS...   **QUINOA**

IF YOU'RE GOING TO DO ONE THING...

Train yourself smart

The next time that your partner or parents complain about your unhealthy obsession with going to play football, insist that you are training your brain, too.

We're not just trying to get you in trouble at home, honest – 24 exercise specialists hailing from 24 different countries have been highlighting the cognitive gains from doing physical exercise.

A report that's appeared in the *British Journal of Sports Medicine* reveals that "a single session of moderate physical activity will benefit brain function, cognition and scholastic performance in children and young people."

In plain English, it means that having a game of headers and volleys with your mates or going to play 5-a-side in your free time could help to improve displays in the classroom or workplace.

The statement goes on to claim that structured or unstructured exercise – such as challenging team-mates to a game of rondos or having a kickabout in the park – will significantly diminish your chances of developing coronary artery disease and diabetes.

If you needed an excuse to go and play football, you've found it.

TRIGGER POINT MASSAGE BALL

The only massages that most of us are familiar with involve health spas, but there is an alternative form of massage therapy available for nursing your body back to life. Trigger point balls perform the same purpose as foam rollers but, coming in various sizes, target more specific areas of the body. This attention to detail comes at a painful price, as they apply greater pressure on muscle tissue – if you've ever had a deep sports massage, you will know what we're talking about. Like foam rollers, these balls have the backing of science: the University of Witwatersrand, in South Africa, tried them out on golfers with poor hip flexibility and found they improved rotation of the joint during a golf swing. Want Mr Messi's liquid hips? Think about giving massage balls a go.

Ryan Giggs used yoga for flexibility, but as we're not all comfortable doing the downward dog in public, FFT chose to compare two gym alternatives instead

1 "Technically it can be difficult to use balls because of their size," explains Gimpel, adding that: "foam rolling offers you a simpler solution."

2 "But because the ball is smaller you can apply more pressure to your aching muscles, so it provides you with a deeper massage."

3 "Time-wise, a ball takes longer to use every session. It's only better if you have a very specific area you want to target."

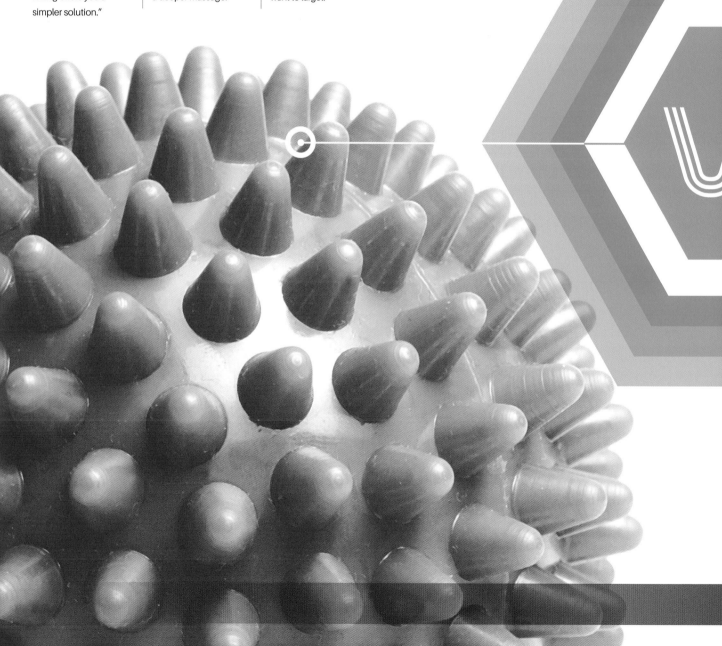

FOAM ROLLER

If you've ever popped down the gym and spotted a balding fortysomething straddling a massive marshmallow, you've probably seen foam rolling. This anonymous-looking piece of gym equipment is used by footballers to massage their lower body before and after training. Rolling sends a signal to the brain to loosen muscles and increase blood flow, to flush out the toxins produced during intense physical activity. This helps to improve flexibility and accelerates recovery.

A study in *Medicine & Science in Sports & Exercise* noted how a foam rolling routine reduced the muscle soreness and increased the range of motion in weightlifters following a squat workout. Think what it could do for your stiff limbs the day after a game.

1 "Our players like them the day after a game as they ease tightness in their legs," reveals Southampton's Head of Performance, Mo Gimpel.

2 "They come in different sizes," continues Gimpel, "but because they're so light, you can easily take any of them on away trips."

3 "Also, foam rollers are easier to use than trigger point balls, and that's because they can massage a much greater surface area."

IF YOU'RE GOING TO DO ONE THING...

Keep your feet on the ground

If you're on the verge of burnout after a hard pre-season - or if you just ache because you're tragically unfit - then Mother Nature may have a simple cure for your woes.

Earthing, a practice that involves the skin touching either grass, sand a river, lake or sea, could accelerate recovery from injury, fatigue and a host of other health problems.

"I've consistently found that earthing offers recovery benefits above and beyond techniques such as icing," said sports chiropractor Jeff Spencer, who has worked in football, basketball and Formula One. "Pain relief is frequently 40 to 50 per cent greater."

Scientists believe that the gentle negative charge that is emitted by the Earth's surface could help to tackle free radicals - molecules which destroy the healthy cells in the body and lead to illness.

A recent study saw 30 patients with sleep issues and muscle and joint soreness report a significant improvement in their symptoms, having each slept on an earthed mattress for a one-month period. So, the next time that you're sprawled out on the physio's treatment table, hop off and tell him you'll lie on the grass instead.

Words Alec Fenn; **Illustration** Alex Williamson

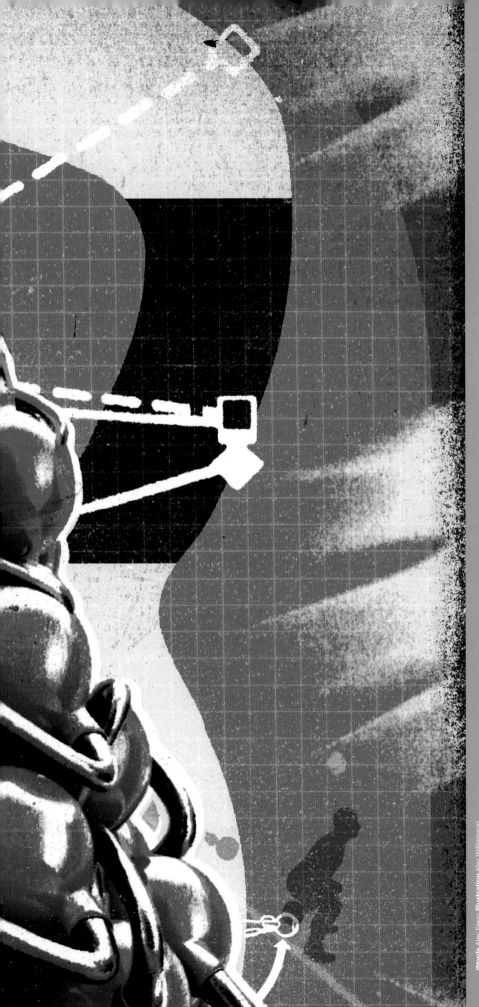

IF YOU'RE GOING TO DO ONE THING...

Get your kettle on

Bored of the bench press and sick of the squat rack? Give kettlebells a go to kick-start your training regime, torch fat and build muscle fast.

The American Council on Exercise have found that a 15-minute workout with those odd-looking metal objects sat in the corner of your local gym can burn as many as 300 calories.

That's all well and good if you want to be Slimmer of the Year, but how will it help you to be a better footballer?

"Kettlebells provide uneven weight distribution, which will challenge and strengthen your core," says strength and conditioning coach Karl Halabi.

"Try some exercises like kettlebell deadlifts and swings. These will use multiple muscle groups, which boosts your testosterone levels and builds muscle, and therefore make you stronger when you're on the pitch."

Don't have any kettlebells lying around at your gym? Well, fear not, because you can even buy them at the supermarket.

Words Alec Fenn; **Illustration** Alex Williamson

Coffee

Caffeine hit

Sports drinks, protein shakes, energy bars – footballers are spoilt for choice if they want a performance-boosting supplement. And yet, a cup of coffee remains the most widely-used legal stimulant among players. It is even claimed that a pre-match caffeine binge could be the difference between success and failure. Dr Rob James, lead researcher at Coventry University, conducted a study which revealed that a very high dose of caffeine improved muscle power and endurance by six per cent. How many times will you need to boil the kettle? The research says 6mg of caffeine per 2.2lbs of body weight – the equivalent of two cups of coffee for an 11-stone male – just before exercise will do the trick. Get yourself down to Starbucks.

If there's one thing footballers love nearly as much as a cheeky Nandos, it's pre-match caffeine. But which of these hot drinks will give you an edge?

1 "Just one cup of coffee [at a size of 8oz/220ml] contains 70-140mg of caffeine – twice as much as a cup of tea," says Holmes.

2 "Coffee increases the levels of the hormone dopamine, which is the key to you improving reaction times and decision-making."

3 "Drinking coffee will also help you to increase your metabolic rate, which will mean burning far more calories at rest."

Tea

Health kick

You can't beat a good old-fashioned cuppa ahead of a game. But tea does more than warm your insides as you take to a muddy pitch in the Sunday morning cold; it helps to keep you in tip-top shape. A Harvard School of Health study revealed the substances called polyphenols that are found in tea can contribute to lowering your risk of developing cardiovascular disease and diabetes. However, if you value your CR7-esque gleaming white smile, drink plenty of water with your Earl Grey. Pigments from dark drinks can become embedded in your tooth enamel, causing discolouration – not what you want when you're smiling with the man-of-the-match trophy.

1 "White and green tea have health benefits as their anti-oxidants prevent cell damage," explains elite sports nutritionist Liam Holmes.

2 "The lower caffeine content found in tea means there's less chance of disrupted sleep which could delay recovery after a match."

3 "Tea will give you a boost but there is far more research showing how coffee boosts mental and athletic performance."

AND OUR WINNER IS... **COFFEE**

ICE BATHS

Long before footballers began jumping into ice baths, the Egyptians were using cold therapies to treat their injuries as early as 2500 BC. Immersing the body in freezing water following exercise will reduce body temperature, blood flow and inflammation, which accelerates recovery. That sounds great, but before *FFT* takes the plunge, is there science to back it up? Er, not really. A study by the University of Auckland in February says it does next to nothing to ease your aching limbs. Professor David Cameron-Smith stated: "Ice baths are no more beneficial than doing a low-intensity warm-down after any intense exercise." We'll stick to a cold post-match pint, then.

1 "If you have a quick turnaround between training or matches, an ice bath could give you short-term pain relief," added Cameron-Smith.

2 "Ice baths can also reduce the benefits of training hard, leading to small gains in strength and muscle mass after doing weight sessions."

3 "Apart from times when you require a very quick wind-down, my advice would be to rule out ice baths from your recovery options."

VS

Which sub-zero remedy will help you to recover quicker during pre-season?

CRYOTHERAPY

Imagine standing inside a giant fizzy drinks can engulfed with freezing cold air hitting temperatures below -100°C, while wearing nothing but your pants. Got it? You have just imagined whole body cryotherapy, which relieves DOMS – delayed onset of muscle soreness – after training and games.

Created by a Japanese scientist in the 1970s, the treatment has been used by Cristiano Ronaldo and Zlatan Ibrahimovic, but the jury is out on its credentials. *The International Journal of Kinesiology and Sports Science* said the alleged benefits of whole body cryotherapy were based on anecdotal evidence due to a lack of large-scale studies. We like a bag of frozen peas anyway.

1 "There isn't enough science to back up the treatment yet, but many athletes believe it helps to relieve stiffness," said Dr Michael Gleiber.

2 "Cryotherapy cools the skin but won't reduce the temperature of your core much in 3-4 minutes, so it is unlikely to reduce inflammation."

3 "The cold will enhance you metabolism, so you burn more calories, bu it isn't a solution to you losing weight."

AND OUR WINNER IS...   **ICE BATHS**

IF YOU'RE GOING TO DO ONE THING...

Keep your chin up

It doesn't matter if you're in the Premier League or Sunday League - the winter period provides one of the toughest challenges during the football season.

Cold weather, rough conditions and bad results can damage team morale and leave you with a crisis of confidence. But you're not alone: even the top pros aren't bulletproof.

Nike Academy psychologist Claire Davidson carried out a study, with 200 players across England's top four leagues answering a survey that measured their resilience. The results showed many professional players admitting they struggled to deal with pressure and setbacks.

"Some players thrive on pressure - like a last-minute penalty - while others will see a tough situation as a threat and they crumble," says Davidson. Yet there is something you can do to bolster confidence.

"Control the controllables," adds Davidson. "You can't control being smaller than your opponent or if you get named on the bench. But you can look for different sources of confidence. Doing some extra training, speaking with another team member to discuss form or changing the way you look at a situation can breed positivity."

Perfect. Perhaps this year *FFT* will avoid our usual goal drought.

Words Alec Fenn; **Illustration** Alex Williamson

FREE WEIGHTS

We can't quite put our finger on why, but there's something manly about holding a pair of rusty old dumbbells in your hands. Plus, strength training using free weights won't just satisfy the alpha male in you – it'll also help to improve your physical performance out on the pitch. A 2008 study in the *Journal of Strength and Conditioning*

Research noted improvements in acceleration, peak sprinting velocity and 40-metre sprint time in a group taking part in strength training twice a week for seven weeks. A further study published in February of this year showed that a group of young footballers who underwent a weights training programme suffered far fewer injuries during a season than a group who did no resistance work.

1 "Free weights' greater range of movement means you'll use more muscles," says strength and conditioning expert Mathew Monte-Colombo.

2 "When you use multiple muscle groups you burn more calories, so you will get a tougher workout with dumbbells or barbells."

3 "Also, compound exercises – squats, deadlifts – strengthen your core. Machines won't, as they're in a fixed position."

VS

Two types of resistance training go under the microscope, as we discover which method works best for improving a footballer's strength

MACHINES

Resistance machines are the lifeblood of the modern super-gym, but can big, flashy pieces of technology really help you to hold your own on a bog of a Sunday League pitch during a bleak midwinter? Well, actually, it turns out they can. In 2008, the University of Saskatchewan in Canada decided to put a controlled group through an eight-week training schedule using just

weights machines and found that knee extensor thickness increased by 4.9 per cent. Strength also improved by an average of 13.9 per cent across the major muscle groups that were trained. The study even showed that levels of testosterone – the hormone you need to build muscle mass – were boosted by an average of 21 per cent during resistance machine workouts. Give them a go and you'll be bursting out of your jersey in no time at all.

1 "Machines are great when a player begins resistance training and needs to build a good base level of strength," says Monte-Colombo.

2 "Some players will struggle to lunge and squat with correct technique, but it's easy to teach a young player how to use a machine."

3 "In injury rehab, machines are good for pinpointing a specific muscle group and slowly adding resistance."

AND OUR WINNER IS...   **FREE WEIGHTS**

Words Alec Fenn; **Illustration** Alex Williamson

IF YOU'RE GOING TO DO ONE THING...

Train on an empty stomach

If you're anything like *FFT*, you grew up with your mum and dad warning you not to skip breakfast or exercise on an empty stomach.

In recent years, however, athletes from a number of sports have opted to ignore those cries and use fasted training to help them lose weight. That list includes four-time Tour de France winner Chris Froome.

"Chris rides in the morning and then has breakfast," former Team Sky nutritionist Nigel Mitchell tells *FFT*. "Leading up to a race, this gets him down to his optimum weight.

"When you wake up, your body's glycogen stores are depleted, so when you train you'll use fat as a fuel and start to lose pounds."

Sounds simple – but could it work for pro footballers who play all year round? And what about amateurs?

"A performance diet and a weight loss diet are very different things," says Science in Sport nutritionist Ted Munson. "If you've got a game in the morning, you will need about 350g of carbohydrates just to fuel yourself for the first half alone.

"But fasted training can be really effective if you go for a morning jog to stay in shape during the week, before your weekend game."

It's time to get running on empty.

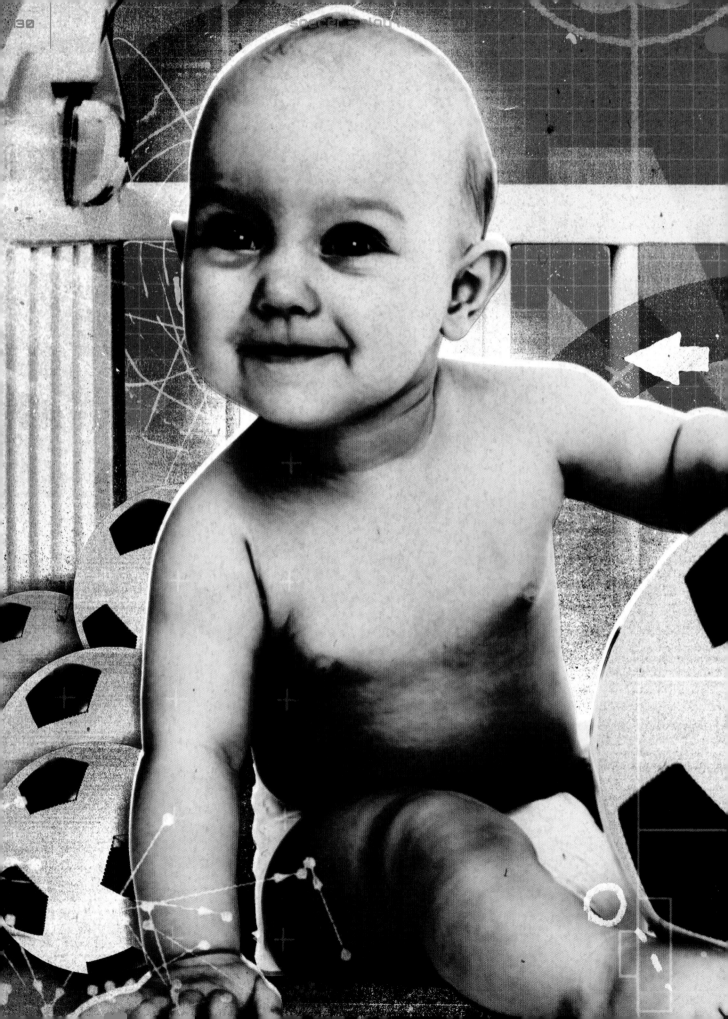

IF YOU'RE GOING TO DO ONE THING...

Coach from the couch

If you fancy yourself as the next Pep Guardiola but don't have the time nor money to study for your coaching badges, we've got good news - you can train up a future star from your lounge.

Tom Byer, world-renowned coach and head technical advisor to the Chinese FA, is the author of *Football Starts at Home*, with his philosophy educating parents about how they can coach their children as soon as they learn how to walk.

"I believe you can start to nurture children's football skills when they are one or two," Byer explained at the Soccerex Football Convention. "Kids should not learn to kick the ball first, they should learn how to roll and manipulate it."

Byer's methods are the result of a 25-year coaching career and he feels that kids must master all of the basics before they join a club.

"Place a small ball in your living room and encourage your child to roll both feet over the ball and then change direction, left and right," he added. "These skills will accelerate their development. Parents are more important than coaches."

But remember – if your little one breaks the TV, you'll get the blame.

Words: Alec Fenn; **Illustration** Alex Williamson

PILATES

Pilates and yoga are the same thing, right? Not quite. Both aim to enhance suppleness but pilates is performed using various pieces of kit – including stretch bands and gym balls – while the exercises all involve a continuous flow of movement, compared to the static positions associated with yoga.

Founder Joseph Pilates created more than 500 exercises, which science has shown are effective at aiding flexibility. A 2004 US National Library of Medicine study found 47 people who did pilates once a week for two months increased their fingertip-to-floor flexibility by an average of 3.4cm. That could be handy when you're picking up the match ball having smashed in another hat-trick.

Dust down the exercise mat to learn which limb-loosening practice is most effective for boosting flexibility

1 "It can be adapted for many positions – forwards can focus on hamstrings to improve speed," stated Pilates instructor Ray Hassan.

2 "The exercises will also help to speed up your muscle and joint recovery after a match – so you will be fit to play another game sooner."

3 "Using resistance gear will improve core strength, which is so important for many of the movements that are related to football."

YOGA

This ancient practice involves posture and breathing exercises that improve flexibility. Manchester United stalwart Ryan Giggs credited yoga with helping him play on into his 40s – and a study last year illustrated exactly how it can aid physical performance. Twenty-six participants went through a 10-week yoga programme that featured two sessions each week, and all of them displayed a significant improvement to their flexibility and balance when performing a range of movements after the programme, compared to their efforts prior to the study. Make it a part of your training regime and you might be able to extend your playing days.

1 "Being supple boosts speed, recovery and sharpness of movement, and yoga improves all of these," said Giggs' yoga teacher, Sarah Ramsden.

2 "Stiff through your hips? It means you could later develop some lower back problems, so doing yoga will help you to get over this problem."

3 "Yoga helps you to transfer power through the core, so you'll move freely and avoid any injuries caused from muscle imbalance."